# Heart Stood Still

# KA HAEA TE ATA

KA HAEA TE ATA

# Heart Stood Still

A conversation about belonging

## Miriam Sharland

OTAGO UNIVERSITY PRESS
Te Whare Tā o Te Wānanga o Ōtākou
otago.ac.nz/press

Based on true events.
This book records stories that I read and heard in 2020.
All sources are given in the Notes.
Some names have been changed to protect privacy.

*This book is dedicated to my mum*

# Contents

# Prologue

How hard it is to escape from places.

—KATHERINE MANSFIELD, Letter to Ida Baker[1]

**I'M AN UNSETTLED SETTLER.** In 2003 I flew away from England on an adventure to establish a new life in New Zealand. But almost seventeen years later I was feeling the threads of family, landscape, home tugging me back. After spending Christmas 2019 in the UK, I realised I didn't want to return to Manawatū. I cried at the airport as I left London and decided to come back as soon as I'd wrapped up my affairs. In January 2020, everything still felt possible.

People sometimes joke that the best thing about Manawatū is that it's easy to get away from, with its central location and multiple routes out. Two months and a global pandemic later, that had changed: no sooner had I made my decision to leave than I was unable to go.

Despite my initial unhappiness at the enforced change in my plans, the strange and unexpected year that followed delivered a gift: time to walk, cycle, notice, think, read and write. I explored places I'd never been to or seen properly, all within a small radius of my house. I noticed the close-up of this region, its texture, weft and warp. Through encounters with others, and by reading, I learnt many stories about Manawatū. And this spurred reflection: on the past, both here and elsewhere; and on my place in the landscape, the consoling power of nature, and what it means to belong.

# Autumn

Soil—Fungi—Fruit

# Soil

One would have thought that with vegetable gardens to tend,
our parents would not have had time for flowers. But flowers,
shrubs and trees we had in abundance ... it is now, looking back,
that I appreciate this more.

—PATRICIA GRACE, 'Waiariki'[1]

**A STATE OF EMERGENCY** is declared at lunchtime. Aotearoa New
Zealand is going into lockdown at 11.59 tonight. I've been isolating
at home alone for four days with bronchitis already, so a workmate
drops off my computer from our office at the university and talks
to me across the driveway. I mostly communicate by nodding and
smiling; I've almost lost my voice. Later, in an online meeting, my
teammates discuss the impending lockdown.

'There's been no flour and pasta for a while,' one says.

I used the last of my flour last week, and I'm too sick to go to the
shops. Anyway, the country has gone into siege mode. Supermarkets
have run out of flour, yeast and pasta. People are fighting over toilet
paper. Food is being rationed. Only four cartons of milk and one bag
of sugar per customer. There is no hand sanitiser to be had.

Being tired and unwell makes me a bit short with my workmates.

'I haven't been to the supermarket for ten days,' I croak. 'Looks
like I'm going to have to forage for acorns.'

Yesterday a colleague left a couple of pastries on my doorstep,
but I hadn't wanted to sit around at home eating junk food and
feeling sorry for myself, so I'd dropped them at the pātaka kai, the

community pantry shelves that have recently been built on the street a block over from my place. Pātaka kai is a grassroots movement to stop food waste and encourage sharing among neighbours to build communities. Its slogan: 'Nā tō rourou, nā taku rourou ka ora ai te iwi / With your basket and my basket we will sustain the people.'[2] Now I wonder if I should have hung on to the pastries.

The *Get Ready Get Thru* earthquake-preparation leaflet has been sitting on my desk for almost a year. Every now and then I'd look at it and think, I really should do that. I flick through it now and note among all the information on how to prepare for an earthquake that it's a good idea to have two weeks' food supply in case of a pandemic. We were all looking in the wrong direction. My emergency food stocks comprise twelve individual Christmas puddings and five jars of artichoke paste bought at knockdown prices from Reduced to Clear.

My friend Karen messages me from England: 'Went to Sainsburys, hardly any tinned products, but apparently no one likes tinned tapioca. BUT I DO! I win!' I tell Karen about the flour, and she says that large amounts of flour can spontaneously combust and maybe the hoarders will blow themselves up.

At lunchtime I make a polenta cake, no flour required. Then my friend Heather rings – she's on her way back from Wairarapa after a last visit to her best mate before lockdown, and she's found 5kg bags of flour in a wholesaler. Would I like some? She drops the flour off at my place later that afternoon, accompanied by a copy of David Malouf's poem 'The New Loaf':

*Each day delivers it*
*new-risen like the sun*[3]

Heather tells me, through the glass barrier of the kitchen window, 'That page fell open. I didn't know the poem, it just arrived at the right time.'

Then we wave goodbye to each other for the last time for a month.

At 6pm I jump as my mobile wails with the national emergency alert that signals the beginning of lockdown. I feel a bit panicky, on the edge of tears, but tell myself out loud to stop being a drama queen and pull myself together.

It's silent when I wake at 6.30am. My chest rattles as I turn over to check messages on my phone. A friend texts, 'Our generation, we thought we were safe.' He's right. Wars and pandemics were things that happened to other people. That was never going to be us. Suddenly, life doesn't seem as certain.

A pandemic could be seen as a kind of war – between humans and a virus. From the virus's perspective, a human body is a home in which it fulfils its life cycle and purpose: replicating its DNA inside the host's cells. Nature always comes down to a battle for survival between organisms competing for resources. Viruses are so good at this that we use them as a metaphor: to go viral – to spread your message to thousands of people in a short time – is the highest measure of success in our digital age. Covid-19 is a reminder that we're not always in control in the way we like to think we are.

My Scottish great-grandmother died of the Spanish flu virus in the Orkney Islands in 1918. She was fifty-five, the age I am now. Her daughter, my Nana, met my Londoner grandad when he was stationed at the naval base in the islands, recuperating from an injury sustained in the trenches. Grandad's Royal Marines discharge papers are marked 'underage'. For him, as for many young men, the war must have represented an opportunity for adventure, a chance to escape a grim and predictable everyday existence. But Grandad's injury was a gunshot wound to a finger on his left hand. Was it the classic 'Blighty', an injury self-inflicted by soldiers desperate to escape the terrible reality of the battlefields? Was Grandad so determined to get home that he turned the gun on himself, even though home is recorded on his discharge papers as '1 Boarded Entry, Wapping' – that is, underneath the arch of a bridge? I wouldn't blame him if he was.

As soon as Nana turned sixteen, they married, and with Nana's mum now gone, Grandad took her back to the poverty of London's East End. Despite being relatively well-off – her father was a master joiner who made coffins for the islanders – Nana had probably been wanting to escape too: from a remote island and a strict Presbyterian upbringing. Grandad, keen to snare this feisty young woman with jet-black hair falling to her waist, hadn't warned her about the squalor of the dockland housing tenements to which they were headed.

Four children – and five miscarriages – followed, including the birth of my mum at the outbreak of World War II. As the Luftwaffe subjected the East End of London to the Blitz, Grandad enforced the blackout as an Air Raid Precaution Warden. Mum's teenage brother joined the army and went off to fight. Mum has vague memories of cowering at dark shapes looming at the window as German bombers flew over, and she's still frightened of loud noises. The war provided another escape route for her mother. The neighbours told her they'd never speak to her again if she left. But Nana was determined to flee, and she evacuated to the Surrey countryside with her three young daughters.

While I'm waiting for my tea to brew, I put flour, yeast, water and sugar into the breadmaker and set it off. Three hours later, the bread machine beeps the rhythm of Beethoven's Symphony No. V. *Da da da daa. Da da da daa. Da da da daa.* V in Morse code. V for victory. On the wall above the breadmaker hangs a poster from the Imperial War Museum in London that says, 'Victory is in the kitchen'. I take the steaming bread out of the machine, spread the crust with butter and take it outside to eat in the sun. Sitting on the bench, looking at my overgrown garden, it occurs to me that victory might be in the garden as well as the kitchen.

Back inside, I look up 'Victory gardens'. Britain's World War II Dig for Victory scheme encouraged people to produce their own food in gardens, allotments and areas of public parks that were dug up for the purpose. Even bomb craters were pressed into service: these abundant, round gardens, some filled with flowers as well as food, were used as a propaganda tool to represent the British people's resilience. Homegrown vegetables nourished the body, while flowers sustained the mind.

An essay by architectural researcher Adam Przywara discusses a bomb-crater garden in the grounds of London's Westminster Cathedral created by a caretaker called Mr Hayes. Przywara comments on how people had forgotten the old patterns of land use and cultivation, which had to be relearnt in the face of wartime food insecurity. Some civilians kept chickens, pigeons, rabbits and pigs. These animals all played their part in the war effort, providing manure as well as meat. Gardeners, Przywara says, had to 'negotiate relations with the soil in times of crisis. Manure became the actor of national importance.'[4] He points out the deep symbolism of Hayes' garden as a human and non-human collective that enabled him to survive the war.

I started gardening enthusiastically when I moved into this place seven years ago, even adding eleven fruit trees to the five that were already on the quarter-acre section, but many of the vegetables I spent hours planting and sowing failed to grow in the tired, hard clay. Last year I didn't bother gardening at all: I was going to be in England over the summer and it was easier and cheaper to go to PAK'nSAVE.

To emulate those victory gardeners, I'll need to start from scratch and renegotiate my relationship with the soil.

Overnight, I learn online about no-dig 'lasagne' gardening. This technique of piling up layers of organic matter to create soil looks like the way to deal with my heavy, stony ground. In the morning I make a start. The vegetable beds have been colonised by oxalis, couch grass and buttercups that ran riot while I was in England. Parsley and borage have self-seeded promiscuously. I grab a fork from the garage and spear it into the soil. Or try to. The ground is like rock. No wonder plants struggled to grow in here. How on earth did the weeds do it? I put the hose on the garden and leave it running slowly.

I walk to the compost pile at the back of the garden; across the school field beyond my gate I see a steady stream of cars on the road and wonder where all those people are going. Next to the compost is the worm farm that I'd left to fend for itself for the six weeks I was away. When I got home, a few desiccated, shrivelled, dark-red worms lay on the top of the soil, but most of them had disappeared – absorbed into the substrate, I assumed. Now I tip it out, breaking up the worm poo that has compacted into a solid lump. Then I see something wriggling … shiny red tiger worms. I carefully pick the worms out and put them back in their black plastic box, then sift through the compost heap for chunks of fruit and veg to feed them. The compost smells like dark chocolate. The pile is studded with plastic: those annoying little stickers from fruit skins; bits of food packaging that blow over the fence from the school field; and tea bags – I read recently that they contain plastic. I salvage corn husks, apple cores and banana skins, put them in the worm farm, top it off with newspaper and pour in some water.

By now the garden bed is wet, and I sink my hands into the earth, extracting stones and weeds. As I work the soil, I stop noticing the light drone of traffic from beyond the school field and hear only birds. Pointed oxalis bulbs with little clusters of bulblets, like buried bombs, wait to create carnage among the neat rows of vegetables I've always hoped for. Tough mint roots snake through the ground, popping up leaves covered in rust pustules. I pull out as much as I can, then rake the soil before loading the beds with compost. I find some old mustard seeds in a tin in the garage and sprinkle them over the brown tilth. A green crop to keep the weeds down and the nutrients in.

Then I build a new bed, laying down cardboard and newspaper over a rectangle of lawn. The paper is open at the gardening page, and I stop to read an article about a UN report that says all the world's topsoil could disappear within sixty years if current rates of degradation continue. The writer concludes: 'If you look after your bit of dirt you may have something to leave to your children that will have more value than gold.'[5]

I pile compost and the remnants of the worm farm onto the paper, then sow seeds that have been languishing in the tin: kale, broccoli, spring onions, peas and red-flowered broad beans. Finally, I fling an old net curtain over the bed to keep the birds off. I am a compulsive hoarder of things that might one day be useful.

I wake up sore and stiff from digging. My chest feels tight and I'm short of breath, so I stay in bed and read one of the books that piled up in my busy pre-lockdown life. In *The Meaning of Birds* Simon Barnes talks about how with the invention of agriculture humans ceased wandering and became settlers, moving from an uncertain but leisurely life to one of security bought through a lifetime of back-breaking labour.[6] That feels about right – my back is killing me. But uncertainty is creeping in again. And while most of us are now settlers, we still have the instinct to wander, even when grounded.

After the war, Nana refused to go back to the London slums, and the family moved into a two-bedroom, semi-detached brick house with a garden, an outside toilet and a blue hydrangea by the living room window. Grandad tried to grow food but, having spent most of his life on the streets of London, he wasn't a natural gardener. Mum remembers him coming home from the pub, lamenting that the local men had laughed at his lack of gardening knowledge. He was more at home drinking with his fellow veterans in the Old Comrades Association Hall. When Mum had us – a son and three daughters, just like her parents, and in the same order – we'd visit Nana and Grandad and have weak orange squash and plain biscuits, while the adults drank strong, sweet tea with evaporated milk.

Grandad stayed in that little house for the rest of his life. I have only vague memories of him: a small, dark, smiling man with kind eyes, sitting quietly in the corner of a gloomy living room. My elder sister remembers being ushered from the room and sent to play in the garden when Grandad started having flashbacks to the trenches, garbling loudly as he hallucinated about mustard gas rolling over. She also remembers our brother biking to meet her as she walked home from primary school in 1975 to tell her Grandad had died. When they got home, Nana was in the living room crying, and Mum was making tea.

Pottering in the garden, I miss the sound of the kids playing on the school field behind my house. I don't have children, but I think back to my 1960s and '70s childhood in the Surrey countryside.

My parents' families were poor. Dirt poor, you could say. They learnt to make do and mend at a young age, and the ethos was passed on to us. Dad's dad was a gardener at a local manor house, and my aunt – the baby of the family – remembers him coming home with a strawberry in each pocket as a treat for her. Dad was taught to garden at the village school he attended until he was eleven, when he was apprenticed as a gardener's boy to one of the big houses in the village. A schoolfriend of Dad's once told me that their education was a blatant servant-creation scheme.

Although our family didn't have money, we did have a large garden. My earliest memories are set there: the little green lizard that crawled out from under the shed to bask on hot stone paving slabs; the hours spent floating back and forth on the wooden swing that Dad built, watching clouds scud across the summer sky, in my pink dress sewn by Mum; the apple trees, whose fruit Mum encased in pastry to make apple dumplings swimming in a pool of sticky syrup. In the earliest photo of me as a baby, taken by Dad, I'm lying on my stomach in front of a flower border, lips puckered as if about to kiss a big coneflower. When we got a bit older, my sisters and I each had a little patch of garden in which Dad showed us how to write our names with flower seeds. In summer, the letters would be patchily spelt out in alyssum, stock, poppies and cornflowers.

Dad was a forester, but after work he dug the vegetable garden or tended plants in the greenhouse, growing lettuces, cucumbers and tomatoes for tea. The pungent, grassy aroma of tomato plants always takes me back there. All my memories of that garden are set in summer, when the six-week school holidays felt like forever. But summer did end, of course, when the sad woodsmoke smell of autumn signalled that it was time to go back to school – and up a year too.

While I was at primary school, Dad had to give up forestry because of a bad back. He turned to selling insurance door to door but wasn't a very good salesman, and soon we moved to a council house in town. Dad got a new job as a postman. When he wasn't trudging the streets delivering mail, he worked the much smaller garden at our new place, still producing lettuces, cucumbers and tomatoes. His garden was not only a means to feed his family but also a way of grounding himself as he moved further away from the woods. Dad died suddenly of a heart attack early one winter's morning when I was seventeen. There was no golden inheritance –

we struggled financially after he was gone – but now I understand that this love of dirt is what he left me.

A message from Karen. She's bought seeds, although she hates vegetables and doesn't like gardening. Celery, parsley and lettuces. Cress, for egg and cress sandwiches. And a bottle of lemon juice in case she gets scurvy. Media here and in the UK report that people are panic-buying seeds, plants and gardening equipment. There's much talk of victory gardens – others are thinking the same way as me. A colleague posts in our work Microsoft Teams app that he's also digging a victory garden and is converting the front lawn into a vegetable bed: 'Food in five weeks. Fresh fruit and produce is going to be "a thing" pretty soon if growers aren't allowed to go out and bring the current crop in.'

Another workmate calls me a hipster for growing kale. This makes me laugh, which makes me cough. I type back, 'Are you kidding? My dad used to grow curly kale – I grew up on it!' And not just kale. Broad beans, peas, carrots, potatoes, cabbages, as well as the salad from the greenhouse.

I spend some time learning more about the local soil. Until fairly recently in geological time, Manawatū was under the ocean. The rock underlying the region is composed of marine sand left when the seas retreated thousands of years ago. Then the climate cooled, vegetation declined and erosion increased. The rivers dropped sediment, forming floodplains. The wind picked up silt and deposited it across the plains and terraces.[7] These particles of rocks and minerals, along with air, water, and the remains of dead plants and animals, make up soil. But soil itself isn't dead; it teems with life. Trillions of creatures dig and till the dirt, composting and recycling its elements, building their own food supply and ours. Soil is a collective.[8]

Te reo Māori has many words for soil. One of them is oneone. Māori academics Jessica Hutchings, Jo Smith and Garth Harmsworth write in *Mai Journal* that oneone has a cosmological dimension, deriving from the first woman, Hine-ahu-one, who was created from clay by Tāne, son of Papatūānuku, the Earth Mother.[9]

Papatūānuku brings forth all things, bestowing blessings on her children. *Te Ara, The Encyclopedia of New Zealand* says Papatūānuku is 'the birthplace of all things and the place to which they return'.[10]

*Te Ara* also says that Māori warriors dying on enemy land after a battle sometimes called for soil from their home to weep over.[11] Reflecting on this makes me wonder when I will stand on English soil again.

I ring Mum and tell her about my gardening. She tells me that after Dad died, she looked at cabbages in the supermarket and wondered how she'd manage: 'I didn't know if we were going to get through it.'

The neighbouring school has a small vegetable garden. I wander through it at lunchtime, looking at the plants: cabbages going to seed, straggly thyme, parsley, onions topped with pompom flowers. Lots of weeds. Slightly guiltily I liberate a small cabbage and a few sprigs of thyme, hoping the kids will be happy that someone is using their crops. After my conversation with Mum, I can't bear for the cabbages to be wasted.

I return in the late afternoon with a trowel. I clear the weeds, plant two rows of broad beans, and sprinkle on the last of the mustard seeds as a cover crop.

Shortly after Dad's death, the council moved us into another house just around the corner. Here Mum started to build a flower garden. As she dug, she hit metal. My brother and his friends took over, excavating old bikes, bed frames and other discarded rubbish that had been swallowed up by the earth. I had my own little patch of ground too, but now I replaced the small flowers that spelt out my name with sunflowers and orange lilies: tall flowers that aimed for the sky.

Today I go to the school field again and talk, from a distance, to a man who turns out to be the caretaker. I explain about the vegetable garden, and he says he'll tell the headmistress that a kind neighbour took care of it during lockdown.

'It's looked after by the Green Team,' he says. 'They'll be really pleased!'

This makes me feel less guilty about the cabbage.

Signs along the school wall spell out 'TEAM: Teamwork. Excellence. Action. Manaakitanga. We take care of each other.' Hutchings, Smith and Harmsworth define manaakitanga as 'the maintenance of whakapapa relationships of reciprocity': you don't grow kai just for yourself but for the collective.[12]

A friend says on Facebook that she's unable to do anything creative, though this is how she's always coped in difficult times. She's spending her time cooking and gardening. I remind her that cooking and gardening *are* creative. It feels as if we're moving back towards survival skills, fostering resilience, negotiating relations with the soil, like Mr Hayes, the cathedral caretaker.

Autumn is often seen as the beginning of the end of the year. But it can also be the start of something. As I look out over the garden this evening, drinking a cup of tea, I ponder that maybe this patch of soil isn't such a bad place to be marooned after all.

# Fungi

Domes of old vellum, and buttons coy and small
White as new gloves

—BASIL DOWLING, 'Mushrooms'[1]

**TO AVOID AIMLESS DRIFTING, I SET A ROUTINE.** Start work early, and at morning teatime take a wheezy walk on the field. I crunch over acorns (I don't need to use them for flour now). A huge puffball fungus, like a half-buried soccer ball, is erupting from the bank, scattering fresh soil.

The day passes slowly. After work, I go back out to the field and sit under a tree to watch the sunset. A cricket chirps. Blackbirds chink and squabble. As the light fades, I spot a man in a dark jacket walking round the track. I get up and go back into my garden, where I feel safer, but hang over the gate, waiting for him to pass.

'Hi.' I wave. He looks at me and says nothing. I wave again. 'Hello.' 'Hello,' he says.

A cold wind blows across the field from the west, and I go back inside.

I need someone to talk to, so I call Karen. It's morning in England. She tells me that a colleague drove her home from work at the beginning of lockdown, then burst into tears before leaving: she lives alone and was dreading the isolation. We discuss the pros and cons of working from home.

Karen describes her first work Zoom meeting: 'Our boss tried to get us chatting. Every now and then people showed their pets ... two cats ... a rabbit ... then there was silence ... so I tried to fill it by saying I had mice. Boss got excited until I said they were vermin. Tumbleweed! Killed the forced conversation dead.'

A friend who also lives alone messages me. No one has contacted her in the couple of weeks since lockdown began, and she's feeling lonely. She's been out fungi foraging; she sends a photo of herself smiling, dog by her side, holding a bagful of huge field mushrooms. My mouth waters at the thought of meaty fried mushrooms.

On my morning walk I find small white mushrooms growing on the school field. I'm not confident in my identification skills but I'm 95 percent sure these are edible. I pick one and send my friend a photo.

'It smells like a mushroom,' I text, 'and it looks like one. But I'm still nervous – they say you shouldn't eat them unless you're one hundred percent sure of your ID.'

They also say that if you eat wild fungi, you should leave some of them so that people will know what killed you.

'Definitely a field mushroom,' she texts back.

I watch YouTube videos on how to ID mushrooms. I'm now 99 percent confident mine is *Agaricus campestris*, or field mushroom, and is edible. I tell my friend I'm going to do a spore print for the final 1 percent.

'Nerd!' she replies.

Before going to bed, I place the mushroom gill-side down on an old envelope. By morning, it has created a beautiful dark-brown spore print. That means it's edible.

I decide to give it a go. I fry it, and it's delicious. I tell my friend I've been brave enough to have a nibble.

'Haven't you ever gone mushroom picking before?' she asks.

It seems odd to me that I haven't. We used to pick blackberries and wild strawberries, and Dad would sometimes come home with rabbits, but we never foraged fungi. Was it because they can be fatal if you eat the wrong one? Or was it their mysterious appearance in dark, damp places, and their association with witchcraft that put us off? My little sister and I used to imagine tiny pixies dancing inside the fairy rings on the common behind our house, and elves living inside the red-and-white-spotted toadstools.

I learn about fungi from mycology websites. The mushrooms and toadstools that grow above ground are the fruit of a larger organism called a mycelium, made up of hyphae – tube-shaped filaments that spread through substrates such as soil, manure or rotting wood. Plants use hyphae to communicate with each other by transporting nutrients and water, and by sending chemical warnings about pests or diseases. Sometimes hyphae run through entire forests in what's been coined the 'wood-wide web'.[2] We're connected to fungi through our dependence on them for beer, wine, bread, medicines and pesticides, as well as the edible mushrooms we get from the supermarket or greengrocer.

I go to investigate the puffball. It's been prised out of the soil and split down the middle; it looks as if it's been used as a football. When I pick it up, the mushroom smell is intense. I take the damaged puffball home, then look at fungi identification sites to work out if it's edible. Apparently, it's more than that: it's *Calvatia gigantea*, the holy grail of fungi finds. The only inedible thing it can be confused with is a football, says one site. So, it's a definite ID. But I'm still a bit nervous. And it looks so much like a human skull, with a stalk attaching it to the soil like a spinal cord attaching a head to a body, that I can't bring myself to eat it. I toss the puffball into the corner of the garden and leave it for the bugs.

Two skinny men sit on a low wall by Memorial Park, a block away from my house, drinking V and smoking. The smoke catches in my sore throat as I walk past, but I smile and say hello. One smiles. The other says, 'Keen for it?'

I laugh nervously, taken aback.

'I mean it,' he says.

'I don't think so.' I keep walking.

'Come on, love,' he calls after me.

The man is probably feeling isolated too, looking for connection, and he's most likely harmless. But I feel angry as I walk on. Now I'll need to find a new walking route to avoid the park.

Sylvia Plath's poem 'Mushrooms' uses fungi as a metaphor for women rising up from obscurity to claim their rights. I like the thought of the mushrooms coming up through the soil, slowly and quietly, to stake their claim to the ground.[3]


On my walk today, I go down to the river, where I find a couple of fungi that look like frilled parasols. I send my friend a picture.

'Any idea what this is?'

'Nah, looks like a deformed field mushroom.'

I look them up when I get home. They're *Coprinus comatus*, or shaggy ink caps, so named because they can be used as ink, but also known as lawyer's wig: non-native, widespread globally, and edible if you eat them when they're young, soon after picking. All the same, I can't quite face them, especially as the larger one has started to liquefy in the plastic bag. I leave the bag on the porch outside, planning to empty the contents into the garden later so they might colonise my front lawn.

In the morning, the liquefied ink cap has left a great black stain on my porch. I try to scrub it off, but it won't budge. If the apocalypse is coming, at least I'll have the means to document it, in mushroom ink, for anyone who may survive.

The clocks go back this morning, and I wake at 4.30. I give up trying
to go back to sleep, get up at five and go for a short, slow bike ride at
first light. I'm gradually recovering from bronchitis, and I need to get
my lungs working again. I puff along but it feels good to be moving.
On my bike, I can keep my distance from people and, I hope, the
Covid virus. The roads are empty. Morning smells fresh and clean.
I watch the sun rise as a skein of geese flies over; the birds circle, then
head off into the sun until they disappear. The geese honk to each
other; they function as a collective, working together for the good of
the group, drafting off each other to save energy and give protection
from predators.

I message Karen when I get home to tell her about the geese. She
says that now when she wakes up early she's going to go for a ride too.

'Probably won't see geese though – more likely to be a fuck load of
mice, but hey ho, still nature, right?!'

We chat for a bit, then she signs off, 'Hugs sweets xx.' She's going
to bed as my day is beginning. Four months ago, when I was staying
with Karen, we could call goodnight across the landing. I miss her.

A friend texts me, offering seeds; I trade peas and kale for spinach
and beetroot. I ride round and pick them up from the doorstep.
Evidence of family life scatters the driveway: basketballs, bikes, shoes.
I text her a thank you, then head towards the community garden
in town for inspiration. But the gardens are gone; a sign on the gate
announces a new housing development. A friend brought me here
for gardening lessons after I bought my house. Lots of migrants had
plots here, and the vegetable beds reflected cuisines of many cultures.
It wasn't just veg though. There were flowers aplenty, and if you
ventured right to the back of the gardens you might spot tobacco.
My friend's plot was a smorgasbord of flowers and vegetables packed
in closely together. Her gardening style was on the wild side: I once
stopped her taking a spade to my lawn.

On the way back, I pass a church that has a sign proclaiming the pandemic is God's punishment for sin. Plagues and epidemics have often been attributed to divine displeasure. I'm not religious – I tend towards paganism – but maybe there's an element of truth in the idea, if nature is your religion. This is Christianity being imposed on a natural event: nature is kicking us back.

Later, I ring a friend who lives next to the community gardens. He's sad that he'll no longer be able to forage apples and plums from the big old trees that have been ripped out. 'If the developers had a brain, they'd leave the mature trees to make the development more pleasant.' A new community garden is being built on the other side of the city, but it won't help the people here. 'I'll miss seeing locals walking back with handfuls of this and that for dinner,' he says.

I go out at dusk. I like walking at this time, as I can see into people's houses. A grey-haired man sits alone at a table in a brick bungalow. An elderly woman does a crossword by the window. Sometimes, glimpses of other people's family lives bring a stab of loneliness: a small boy sitting under a red lantern; a young woman drinking wine in a kitchen while a man bends into the fridge.

Good Friday. I wake at 6.30 and pull the curtains. Even though it's light, this week's full supermoon is still clear. I want to get outside and look at it.

A woman is power walking round the field. I've seen her before, in the neighbourhood fruit and veg market that used to run on Saturday mornings, before lockdown.

'Good morning!' I call to her.

'Good morning! Nice day. So quiet!' she replies.

'Beautiful,' I say. 'Look at the moon!'

I'm not sure the woman hears or understands me: although she nods, she doesn't look up. I look down. I've become obsessed with fungi. I scour the ground on my circuit round the field but find only a couple of field mushrooms. As I pass the woman again, she calls out, 'Hey, hey!' and points to the ground. On the edge of the track, a little puffball is breaking through the soil. It looks like a tiny brain. I laugh and thank her. It's too small to pick, so absurdly I cover it with a leaf when she's passed so as not to hurt her feelings.

I fry the mushrooms for breakfast; they're dark and rich and intensely flavoured. I've been missing out on these treasures, and now I have a taste for the hunt. I decide to widen my search. I go out on my bike at lunchtime. At the old gasworks drain that runs from the road onto the cycle path, a mountain bike lies on the ground and a stocky man is bent over in the ditch. I glance over and see it's a friend. He's gathering watercress – great green clouds of it fill the drain. I tell him I'm off to find mushrooms, and he stands up quickly.

'Where?'

'Wherever I can find them!'

Small puffballs punch through the tarmac in the edgeland between road and berm. On the river path I get off my bike and walk with my eyes downcast. I find a big cluster of shaggy ink caps in the grass. I've brought a paper bag especially for collecting – I've learnt that fungi don't liquefy in paper as they do in plastic bags – and pick some younger ones. A jogger I've seen here a few times runs past, moving to the other side of the track as she says hello. I hold up a shaggy ink cap.

'Oh, that's what you're looking for!' she says. 'But are they mushrooms or toadstools?'

I tell her they're edible mushrooms.

'The worst that can happen is you get a happy mushroom,' she says, widening her eyes as she jogs off. Then she calls over her shoulder, 'There's some by the bin.'

I ride up to the car-park bin to have a look, but there are only two mushrooms and one has been nibbled by bugs. I continue through the village and slog up the hill, gasping for breath. I stop at the top to cough, blow my nose and get my breath back, and am rewarded for my effort by a berm covered with mushrooms in various stages of development. It doesn't look as if anyone has been picking them, so I fill two carrier bags with the bounty.

Back on the main road, I scan the roadside as I ride slowly, looking for more. There's one! But no, it's a coffee cup lid. Others turn out to be stones and a scrap of white fabric shredded by a lawnmower. But then, bingo – another patch. My ride home takes twice as long as usual, but by the time I get back I have mushrooms to share. I ride round to my watercress-gathering friend's place, leave a bag outside his door and text to let him know it's there. It feels odd, this distancing. Normally I would go in and chat, be engulfed in a warm hug, get some kai. He never lets me leave empty-handed. The first time I visited, I took homemade plum jam. I left with fruit mince tarts.

On the way home along the river I stop by a large conifer, check that no one is looking, then give the tree a hug, laying my cheek against the rough bark, inhaling its spicy scent, feeling its life force, happy to touch something that's alive.

Jelly ear fungus (edible, but chewy and tasteless, not recommended for dinner by mycologists) has sprouted in the mulch in the new garden bed. Self-seeded spinach, mustard greens and coriander pop up in the other vegetable patches, descendants of plants that lived here in the past. I like this riotous tangle of growth and free food, so I decide to leave it, even though my newly sown vegetable seedlings will have to compete.

I get out of bed when I hear the birds start to sing, and slowly ride down to the river. Slug trails sparkle in the morning sun. At the end of the path a man kicks a broken Corona bottle off the tarmac. The car park is graffitied with black rubber tyre marks from burnouts and donuts. I stop to help, and we discuss vandalism, spite, boy racers, and the council's plans to develop the fields here for housing as a 'solution' to the problem of anti-social behaviour. Then we talk about the ugliness of the developments of large houses creeping across Manawatū.

'So many people live alone now. Why don't they build nice, small houses?' I say, and he agrees.

There's something communal about my first human interaction of the day, despite our despair at the region's problems.

Talk in the media is of isolation, lockdown, distancing. But outside, people are opening up, coming out of their houses, walking the streets, smiling at each other and asking after the health of strangers. I meet neighbours I didn't know I had, talk to people who live on my street whom I've never seen before. New connections are forged. People are walking, running and cycling. In Manawatū we're lucky to have space, most of us, and low Covid rates. People across the country have put teddy bears in their windows so children can follow a bear hunt when they go out. The bears make me feel less alone. People care. We are a community.

This morning the same woman is walking on the field. We stop to chat as we pass each other, one on either side of the path. She doesn't speak much English, but she tells me she's from China, and I tell her I'm from England. She lives in the white house on the other side of the school. I ask her if she works at the market, and she says she goes there to buy vegetables. I think she says she looks after her grandchildren, but then she tells me they've gone to Auckland. I get the impression she's lonely. We move on, in opposite directions, and when I reach my gate again I wave goodbye and go back inside to work.

Anzac Day. The Dawn Service at the war memorial is cancelled, so I stand outside my house at 6am. As my eyes grow accustomed to the darkness, I see people standing all the way down the street.

After breakfast I put a teddy in my bike panniers, his head poking out the top, and go for a ride round the neighbourhood. Poppies, crosses, wreaths and 'Lest we forget' signs are everywhere, alongside or even adorning the teddies.

On through the market gardens outside the city, where orderly rows of cabbages are marked with white plastic sticks. No weeds here. An elderly man walking at the side of the road looks around when he hears my bike.

'Good morning!' I call out.

'Hello! Isn't it lovely?'

'It's gorgeous.'

I'm one of the lucky ones, I know. The pandemic has been terrible, fatal, for many people, especially overseas. The casualty numbers continue to mount in the UK. But here, autumn has been glorious, and although I've missed my friends and workmates, I've loved the traffic-free roads, peace, clean air, and feeling part of a community that cares. I'm optimistic things are going to get better.

Anzac Day is a reminder to enjoy life while you can because you never know what's coming.

Sunday. The last day of level four lockdown. It's overcast, cloudy, windy, and the afternoon is strangely quiet. A back-to-school feeling hangs over the city.

I wake to the alarm at six, feeling cold; the first thing I hear is traffic. An unexpected, small part of me feels comforted by the vehicle noise. We've made it. A return to normality. The feeling doesn't last long. At lunchtime I ride to Bledisloe Park: there are so many cars. The traffic seems worse than pre-lockdown, but maybe I'd just been used to the noise and pollution.

Heather messages me: 'I didn't seem to get the memo saying level three means stop walking and biking and get back in your car.'

I see a flush of what I think are wood boletes, some of which have been knocked over. Is the irresistible urge to kick mushrooms just a destructive human impulse, or is it the fungi's way of enlisting us to spread their spores?

I stop at a picnic table by the stream. A tiny, perfect fly agaric grows in the roots of the tree against which I lean my bike. I plonk down on the bench for a snack. Leaves whirl down furiously in the wind. Something heavy falls and bounces off the table – a conker maybe. Perhaps I should put my helmet back on. Under the birch trees dark-brown mushrooms rot into the soil. Next to them, a dead rat and several fungi I don't recognise, but white-gilled, so probably poisonous. Nature suddenly doesn't seem so benevolent.

On the way back from a walk with my buddy Kerstin we drop in to see a friend of hers. We chat on the doorstep, and she points out a ring of fungi in the lawn that she dislikes and doesn't know how to get rid of.

'There was probably a tree here,' I say.

'There was a tree here! But we took it down. It's astonishing that you know that.'

She seems to be wondering at my knowledge as if it's some kind of witchcraft, so I explain about the wood-wide web, how the mycelium is a superhighway disseminating information through the natural world. She likes the analogy, marvels at how fungi and trees work together, and I see annoyance turn to connection.

'Why don't you leave it?' I ask. 'You may get some fairies dancing in it at midnight.'

I'm still working from home, and by lunchtime I'm going stir-crazy. I ride to Linton Army Camp where four helicopters hover in the air like dragonflies. The sound of gunfire and chainsaws echoes. A new sign says: 'Defence Force property. Due to Covid-19 only Defence Force staff and their families may enter. All other people turn around.'

I ride back to the university arboretum along the river path. Usually it's deserted when it's raining. Today there are loads of walkers and cyclists. Despite them, I feel lonely.

The rain gets heavier. At the arboretum I lean my bike against a tree, then creep into the bush and sit on a stump under a tree fern that forms a natural umbrella. I'm dry and cosy in my hoodie and waterproofs. Time slows down, but I don't get my phone out. Lately I've been feeling that I've become so addicted to machines and screens – working on a computer, shopping online or at supermarket self-checkouts, communicating by mobile phone, constructing images of myself through social media posts, running and cycling indoors while following my progress on apps, relaxing by watching television – I've lost track of what's real. Looking at a phone is a solitary activity, but here, in the bush, I see beyond my isolation and find society in the natural world.

The sheltering fern grows from the rotting stump of another tree: the dead supporting the living. I'm surrounded by kawakawa shrubs, their leaves riddled with holes from the kawakawa looper moth caterpillar, which eats nothing else. I push over a small white toadstool – white gills, definitely not edible. Tiny, bright orange fungi grow over a fallen branch. I rest my head against the fuzzy trunk and close my eyes for a few minutes. I could fall asleep right here and become grown-over with fungi myself. After a few minutes I open my eyes, examine the tree trunk and peel off a piece of bark. A fat grey caterpillar coiled up behind it falls out and lands on my foot. I'm momentarily repulsed, then feel guilty for disturbing it and damaging the tree. I notice cleavers stuck to the Velcro of my waterproof pants. Even now I'm wrecking habitat, disturbing insects and carrying seeds that might run amok in the bush. It's so hard to tread lightly.

The rain eases off, so I ride further into the arboretum, parking under a fig tree. There's hardly anyone here, but I'm not alone. A blackbird watches me, and a piwakawaka flits close by, looking for food. Fly agarics the size of dinner plates grow under beeches. I'm hungry for new mushroom experiences, so I take snaps of the boletes beneath the birch trees to send to my fungi-picking friend, hoping she'll tell me they're edible. I'm so distracted by a forest of tiny rust-coloured toadstools in the grass that I walk into a camellia bush. I pick one of its white blooms, symbol of the Suffragettes.

A yellow-lichened plaque at the foot of a tree reads:

*In loving memory of Ngaire Batchelar*
*1938–1994*
*A staff member who loved these gardens.*

I sit next to Ngaire for a while, watching sunlight filter through the golden leaves of tall trees I can't name. The song of a thrush echoes around the sky. *Let it go, let it go,* says the bird, and I realise I can't stay angry forever. I find a measure of peace away from the hubbub of 'back to normal'. The disappointment at our seeming to have rejected the possibility of a shift to a different way of living starts to ebb.

Back home, I put the camellia in a jam jar, then google Ngaire, of whom I find no mention, except that she's buried in Kelvin Grove Cemetery on the other side of the city. But I do find other Batchelars in online archives. Various sources recount the story of John Octavius Batchelar who, like my mum, was a Cockney. In 1866, aged twenty-six, he emigrated to New Zealand and married Elizabeth Davidson. The couple ran the Royal Hotel, which still stands; it frequently hosts metal concerts. But town life was too rough for Elizabeth, who hated the men who drank away their wages in the hotel bar and then fought in The Square. So Batchelar bought land across the river from Rangitāne, planted it with willows and built a home named Willowbank. The government bought the Batchelar Estate in 1926, after the couple's deaths, to house Massey Agricultural College (later University).[4] Willowbank was demolished in 1980. Perhaps Ngaire felt some familial connection to this place, and that was why she loved these gardens.

Massey's first principal, Professor Geoffrey Peren, turned the land from sheep grazing to an arboretum. He wrote to tree enthusiasts, park managers and plant collectors around the world, requesting specimens. But former Massey head gardener Dave Bull was the real force behind the arboretum as it appears today. Bull worked at Kew Gardens in London, then studied horticulture at Massey. In the 1980s he developed the current arboretum (using straw from Massey Vet School as mulch – here are animals playing their part in garden creation again).[5] Bull's gardening ethos was described in a 1991 Massey newsletter: he filled the area next to the main campus road with early-flowering rhododendrons and other plants that bloom at exam time to cheer despondent students.[6]

Manaakitanga: Mr Bull, taking care of the students' souls.

Through the window I see the Chinese grandmother doing laps of the field, so I go out to walk with her. She waves to me with both hands as I come through the gate. When I catch up to her, we walk together but apart. I tell her my name, and she says her daughter is called Miriam too. Her name is Shelley. I walk with gloved hands in my pockets. Shelley indicates, miming, that swinging your arms is good exercise.

'My hands are too cold!' I tell her.

She says it will warm them up, then comes closer, grasps my hand, and laughs: her fingers feel warm against mine.

# Fruit

Ladder against a plum tree is code
for jam.

—JENNY BORNHOLDT, 'Peach, the Jam'[1]

**I'M RELUCTANT TO GO TO THE SUPERMARKET:** too much risk of picking up Covid on top of the illness that still lingers in my chest. I don't want to take an online shopping slot from someone who needs it more than me either. Although friends are helping with shopping, getting fresh produce remains an issue until my lungs fully recover and my vegetables grow.

I cycle through the market gardens. With an increase in traffic has come an increase in litter, mostly drink cans, plastic bottles, takeaway cups and food containers. A passing SUV bears a sticker saying 'HUNT GATHER PROVIDE'. A harrier feasts on a dead rabbit. A white ute approaches: the top predator. Another freshly killed rabbit looks at me with a glassy stare. I contemplate putting it in my panniers to eat later, but I've never skinned an animal and the thought repulses me. Things aren't that bad.

Men pick cauliflowers in the fields. I want to ask if I can buy one, but the workers are too far away to hear me and I'm reluctant to approach people. Outside a house stands a bucket of feijoas and a sign saying 'Free – Help Yourself'. A woman shovels horse manure from the berm; she waves as I pass. I pull over to have a look at a fruit and veg stall: paper bags of feijoas $5. Two limes $1. Eggs $7 a dozen. An old tin has been fashioned into an honesty box, still with the label: 'Clean and lean shake. Vanilla flavour.' A replacement for real food. I buy some eggs and put them in my panniers, hoping they won't get shaken around too much.

A burnt-out car seat litters the entrance to the river path at the next village, Ashhurst. A hare runs through the field alongside the path, then ducks through the fence, crosses in front of my bike and disappears into the bush. I lift my feet and freewheel through a brown puddle. A flock of sparrows, fifty or more, rises up from gleaning in a shorn field, and twists around me. I stop to gather a handful of late blackberries. My jogger friend passes.

'They're few and far between now,' she calls over her shoulder. 'Just enough to go in a smoothie.'

But in truth, there's not enough even for that. It's not worth carrying them home, so I eat as I pick. The sun's come out and it feels hot through my leggings. The bank is covered in dying bindweed, and I wonder if the council sprays here. I eat the blackberries anyway; they're sweet and musky, with no chemical hint of pesticide. A branch higher up the bank has a spray of ripe berries; I reach up and manage to grab the branch by a leaf and pull it towards me. As I snatch a handful of berries, a particularly vicious branch catches me by the scruff of my cycling jacket. With one foot planted in the bank, I rip myself away from it, hoping I haven't torn my jacket. I've become obsessed with the hunt. When we were kids, wild blackberries were a valuable free food source. Brambling trips were a late-summer-into-autumn ritual; scratched hands, purple-stained fingers and sunburnt calves are some of my most vivid childhood memories.

As I think about Mum's homemade bramble jelly, a large red-faced man, bare-chested, with his shirt tied around his head, marches towards me. He seems slightly aggressive, and I straighten up, but he stops a few feet away.

'You know these are a noxious weed here?' His accent is Irish.
'A delicious noxious weed!' I reply.

'Me Ma used to make them into blackberry turnovers,' he says, softening. He pauses for a minute, looking at the hedge, then walks away, murmuring as he goes: 'Blackberry turnovers ...'

The weather looks like it's going to turn again, so I don't hang around. There's a rare easterly, so I fair fly back with the wind behind me. Halfway home, fat raindrops start to fall. The light is intense. A rainbow arcs over the ranges. Emerald grass, a chestnut horse, a glossy black cow; far off in the field of cauliflowers, a red tractor like a toy left by a giant child. The white wind turbines spin on the ridge. Rows of tiny celery plants resemble neat green embroidered sprigs on brown fabric. Brown and white, and black and white cows lie down in a field. Shocking-pink dahlias cluster around the base of a telegraph pole, escapees from a field of regimental rows of blooms in the neighbouring field.

On the main road a bike lies on the grass and a woman picks apples from a tree overhanging the ditch. I've been eyeing this tree up, uncertain if I could clamber over the ditch safely, not sure whether it's on someone's property or growing wild at the side of the road. The woman smiles at me slightly self-consciously; perhaps she's been grappling with the same questions. I smile back, happy to see her rescuing the apples.

Later, Heather rings for a chat. She tells me her family stopped picking blackberries in Otago, where she grew up in the 1970s, when the council started spraying them with herbicide.

It's my nephew's nineteenth birthday. My elder sister reports from England that he has Covid but is well enough to get out of bed and eat cheesecake.

This morning I walk to Memorial Park. The park is dedicated to those who served in the armed forces, and people who have died or been injured at work. Rosemary grows along the edge of the path, for remembrance. The public toilet is painted with a World War II-themed mural: tea-ration coupons form the background to women painting stocking seams on their legs.

Back at home, I make a pot of tea: two English Breakfast, one Earl Grey. I hesitate as I put the third teabag in – should I start rationing? I decide I don't need to scrimp, and I make my usual strong brew.

At the outbreak of World War II, Britain imported most of its food. The Germans immediately targeted shipments coming from the British colonies: destroying food convoys has always been an effective war strategy. The country was physically isolated. The government introduced rationing in 1940 to ensure everybody got enough to eat: sugar, butter, meat, tea, margarine, cooking fat, cheese and jam all went 'on the ration'. Not wasting food was going to be crucial for the war effort. Rationing was also designed to stop profiteering through inflated prices.[2] In New Zealand, petrol was rationed as soon as World War II was declared, and food restrictions began in 1942, with sugar the first item on the list. But New Zealand didn't suffer the same food shortages as Britain: the rationing policy here was intended to create a surplus that could be sold to the Allies. Tea was restricted to 60 grams a week – enough for three cups a day.[3] I get through that much before breakfast.

In the evening I call Mum. She's made rhubarb and orange crumble with rhubarb from my elder sister's garden and tinned oranges.

'Tinned mandarins?' I ask. I haven't eaten those since I was a kid.

'Yes, I thought I'd be more adventurous, not just make the same old thing Mother used to make.'

I ask what that was.

'Poor old Mother, she never had any ingredients to cook anything different with, and she was a lousy cook anyway. Bread pudding, bread and butter pudding, suet roly poly with dried fruit, macaroni with milk, rice pudding.'

'Fruit and vegetables weren't rationed but there was never much about. We never saw peaches or nectarines. We never had bananas and custard because there were no bananas. If word got around that there was a shipment of bananas coming, people would queue – great long queues outside the fruit and veg shop. They limited the number, so Mother would send me and Pat [Mum's sister] to stand separately in the queue and we'd get two bananas each.'

Mum and her siblings would find an orange at the bottom of their Christmas stockings as a treat: a tradition our family continues.

There's a house on my street with a big mandarin tree in the front garden. Year after year, the mandarins rotted on the grass. Then a family of Bhutanese refugees moved in; I stopped one morning to talk to the woman who often stood at the gate, waving as I biked past, and she gave me some fruit. The family has gone now, and the citrus are uneaten again.

The young men who have taken over the house are often outside tinkering with their cars. Today as I walk past one of them is on the driveway, under the bonnet. I call over to him from the footpath and ask if I can pick some fruit.

'Help yourself. They just get wasted.' He reminds me of my nephew.

'Don't you eat them?' I ask.

He shakes his head.

'You should, they're good for your immune system.'

He gives me a look that says he doesn't want an auntie-style lecture, so I tell him I'll go and get a bag and come back.

'Yeah, that's fine,' he says.

I come back, pick three carrier bags of fruit, call out thanks, and he waves as I go. I drop a bag at my neighbour's door, then walk to a friend's place and leave some on the porch.

The scent of mandarins fills the house, like an English Christmas.

The city is awash with feijoas. I have two feijoa trees, but I can't stand the fruit. I distribute mine to friends and neighbours and put a couple of bagfuls in the pātaka kai.

I wonder if there's something I can make with feijoas that would disguise their pungent taste. While I'm searching (fruitlessly), I learn that, despite the Kiwi-sounding names of new varieties such as 'Kakapo' and 'Pounamu', feijoas were introduced to New Zealand in the early 1900s from South America, where they grow wild in the mountains.[4] Like the tea that was imported from India and China to Britain, and became a symbol of Britishness, feijoas have become symbolic of New Zealand's landscape, culture and cuisine. They are both local and exotic.

I walk around the block; there are quite a few people about. With my hacking cough I'm a social pariah. When I splutter, people look at me and move further away. I take in the queue of people outside the supermarket and can't face joining them.

I pause at a big old fig tree in a park near my house to watch a silvereye feast on insects. The bird lifts its wing with a flash of green. A blackbird hops around the inside of the canopy, unperturbed by my presence; he's not going to be scared away from his meal. I skirt the outside of the tree, picking my share of almost-ripe figs in the sunshine, my hands growing sticky with white sap.

At home, I put half the figs on a plate near the windowsill to ripen, then I turn the rest into chutney.

Out at the science park, a camellia hedge is covered in intense pink blooms, like a Karl Maughan painting.

At a little grove of nut trees, I fill bags with windfallen walnuts and chestnuts. As kids, we picked chestnuts from the trees on the common. Dad stamped on the prickly cases and we'd throw the extracted nuts in the fire until they burst with a loud crack. Sometimes they'd shoot out of the fireplace, burning small holes in the fireside mat and startling the cat from her sleep.

On to the arboretum. I park my bike by the bridge, then wade through long, wet grass to pick small, tangy cider apples from neglected trees. The arboretum smells like the cellar of the old cider house in England where I used to pull pints as a student. The landlord told me that the secret ingredient of scrumpy cider is a dead rat in the barrel, but maybe he was pulling my leg.

I walk to the russet and gold medlar tree, whose fruit hangs out of reach on higher branches. I clamber up the wet bank and give the tree a shake, loosening some hard brown fruit, which I add to my bag. My feet are freezing, so I walk back to my bike, picking up vibrant vermillion and yellow heart-shaped leaves as I go, shaking off the tiny creatures that crawl across them. I load the panniers with my haul and wobble home.

I haven't eaten medlars before, so I look up how to cook them. They're called 'cul de chien' in France, which translates as 'dog's arse'. They're not pretty, and you can't eat them until they've rotted (or bletted), which breaks down tannins and increases sugar content. This doesn't sound promising, but I decide to give the medlars a go. I put them in a dish and leave them on the table to blet. Then I turn the apples into sauce and fill jars ready for winter.

It's raining feijoas. No matter how many I pick up, there are always more lying beneath the trees. I gather a bagful to take to the pātaka kai. It takes me a while to cross the street that was almost empty of traffic this time last week. I offload the feijoas and take a butternut squash from the pile on the shelf that seems to be constantly replenished, like the magic porridge pot in the fairy tale.

Mushroom season is over, but there are plenty of ripe figs at the park, warmed by the late-autumn sun, and I fill a bag with soft, purple-green fruit. A discarded plastic Coke bottle under the tree fills me with disproportionate rage.

I go out to walk round the school field at dusk. A large flock of ducks flies over, then comes in to land on the far side. I count thirty-one of them. They're so elegant in flight, but on the ground they waddle comically. The ducks head towards the oak trees, where they sift the grass with their beaks for acorns. As I get close, the whole flock takes off, and the birds fly towards the evening star with a whirring of wings.

The ducks reappear every day, beating the bounds of the field, just before the sun goes down. Watching them becomes an evening ritual.

A flight of white doves pours down the street ahead of me as I ride through the neighbourhood, then lands on the road, using the tarmac as a runway. Doves are pigeons with fancier coats and better metaphors.

The birds walk onto the grass to feed on fruit fallen from the trees that line the street. I follow their lead and pick some too. Back at home, I search the internet and discover the trees are dogwood, or Himalayan strawberry, and that the fruits are edible. This is another new flavour for me; the tree strawberries taste like mild, sweet custard.

At the university, japonicas lie scattered at the bottom of prickly bushes around the car park of the food science buildings; I gather a bagful to add fragrance to stewed apple, scratching the back of my hand as I reach for them. A persimmon tree by the empty student accommodation is hung with perfect orange globes. I pick half a dozen and put them in my backpack, then take one more and bite it; it's so astringent my teeth fur up instantly and stay that way until I get home and brush them. I look up persimmon and find that they too have to be bletted before they can be eaten raw, so I put them in a row along the kitchen windowsill.

About five o'clock I walk round the field, waiting for the ducks. It's dusk already – where are they? I feel slightly anxious. But then they appear. Three early-birds, then two more. My neighbour is running on the track; he calls to me, 'Here come the duckies!' The small advance party swoops back and forth over us, then the main force comes up from behind the trees. The two groups merge and circle a couple of times before landing on the soccer pitch and rushing on awkward webbed feet to the acorns.

The garden smells of autumn: leaf mould, rotting vegetation, fermenting fruit. Around the trees, worms pull fallen leaves into the soil to recycle into humus. All manner of seedlings have sprouted in the vegetable beds, their seeds shovelled in with my homemade compost or blown in on the wind. I can't identify them all, but predict they'll be edible or pretty, or both, so I leave most of them be. There are poppies that will mature into dramatic dark-purple double blooms; orange California poppies that have spread through the garden from the wildflower seed a friend gave me two Christmases ago; borage with its pale-mauve flowers and prickly leaves; blue forget-me-nots; bright green parsley and coriander. And a whole new generation of oxalis with its lemony leaves. The weeds will hold the soil together over winter, too, when the rain comes.

I'm outside for a while, immersed in the garden, and know when it's five o'clock, because the ducks fly over.

A friend gives me a bag of Granny Smith apples from the supermarket. I'm grateful, and the apples are crunchy and sweet, but there's something slightly alien about their uniform size, shiny green waxed skin and plastic stickers now that I'm used to the misshapen, intensely flavoured apples from the orchard.

The medlars are ready. I scrape the squidgy brown flesh into a bowl, add water and cinnamon, and bake them. In half an hour, they're meltingly soft, slightly grainy, spicy and delicious. The persimmons aren't such a success: they're bland and a bit slimy, so I put them in the worm farm.

I speak to Mum this evening and tell her about the fruit.

'Sounds like paradise,' she says. 'Your dad would have loved it. Still, you're living it for him.' Then she adds, 'I feel sorry for your dad; he never lived to see the good times.'

Covid seems to be in retreat: 'We may have won a few battles, but we have not won the war,' the prime minister says.[5]

The state of emergency is over, bringing some freedom of movement. I'm feeling a lot better, so I drop into my favourite café in town for a coffee, a fruit muffin and a chat with the owner. He says New Zealand must open its borders again or it risks becoming a banana republic.

'A feijoa republic,' I say.

Things may go back to normal soon. But I feel different. I used to go op-shopping on Saturday mornings, but now I know I didn't need any of that stuff I bought. I was just filling in time.

Saturday. The op shops are open again, but I go for a walk. Council workers blow leaves out of the woods with petrol-powered leaf blowers. A shirtless man walks past me. It's hot, and I'm overdressed; I long to take my tee-shirt off too, and throw my arms up to the sun.

I stop at the fig tree on the way home. The figs have nearly finished; I pick the few remaining small green fruit and spend the afternoon boiling figs and sugar. By evening the pantry is reassuringly lined with jars of jam and chutney. I send Karen a photo and tell her I'd survive an apocalypse with my new-found free-living skills.

The nights are getting cooler: I'm feeling the change of seasons more acutely this year. Just as some animals store up food for winter, I'm getting ready for the cold and dark time to come. This abundance will see me through.

# Winter

## Water—Star—Stone

# Water

A river is never silent. Even its
deepest pools thrive with dark
or dreamy utterance. They shelter
more than we can say we know.

—BRIAN TURNER, 'Listening to the River'[1]

**METEOROLOGISTS HAVE PREDICTED** a warm start to winter, and it is indeed mild – and wet. I haven't felt like going for a long ride in the couple of weeks since level two lockdown kicked in – the traffic has put me off, and it's been grey and miserable. But lack of movement is making me twitchy, so I head out for a cruise around town despite the weather.

Today is World Bicycle Day. As I wait to cross the main road in pouring rain, a low-slung black car does a U-turn at the junction and accelerates away. In its back window a sticker says, 'Fuck cyclists'.

Recently a young motorcyclist died after hitting a car near here at speed. An eyewitness said the motorbike was doing nearly three times the speed limit. A cross has appeared on a streetlamp; underneath it, plastic flowers serve as a transient monument.

'Slow down, Slow down', flashes the speed sign.

The city shimmers with car lights; the sky looks like a bruise. My house feels like sanctuary when I get home. It's only 3.15, but the blackbirds are chit-chit-chitting already, it's that dark.

Evening. Teeming rain. It's unusually still. I go for a walk, and woodburner smoke catches in the back of my throat. When I get home, my hair and jacket stink. Standing at the window, I watch rain drip from a streetlight.

A friend rings. 'What will you do,' he asks, 'if the situation is exactly the same this time next year?'

The truth is, I don't know. My life doesn't seem to be under my own control anymore.

I wake to the sound of a plane. Rain. Traffic. A cyclist friend phones, raging about the number of cars now lockdown has ended.

Over the garden fence I see a mini peloton of bike helmets pass by. The small number of children who are back at school are riding round the bike track. Their teacher pootles along behind on a mountain bike. A flurry of wet, pink blossoms blows towards them from my camellia tree.

I'm feeling tetchy, fretting about work, Mum, the planet, so I get my bike out too. I go to town and pick up library books. With a newfound interest in this region, I select books from the local history section.

Next, I head to a new bike shop opening where a friend tells me a cyclist has been hit on a roundabout; he saw the crumpled bike on the road, an ambulance, police cars. After the quiet streets of lockdown, I feel increased anxiety about being injured or killed on the road. I weave nervously home through queues of cars. The hope I'd had for lasting change after lockdown seems ever more naïve and idealistic. The pandemic forced us to slow down, but only temporarily. We've sped up again, back to the normality of constant motion. I know what this means for the planet – but how does that square with my desire to fly to England? The feeling of being grounded returns, alongside the fear of being a hypocrite.

As I roll into my driveway, a thrush sings from the top of the tangled old plum tree that divides my front garden from my neighbour's. Its song reminds me to focus on the things that make me happy. I make tea and sit by the french windows, looking out over the garden. A blackbird in the apricot tree shakes its tail feathers to dislodge raindrops. Its orange beak is the same gold as the leaves that drop from the tree, where a tiny, perfect bird's nest sits in the crook of a branch.

I feel flat and headachy, and don't get out of my pyjamas until 10.30. I can't focus on work and end up cleaning the pantry. About midday I kick myself into action and go out for a walk.

The island separating east- and west-bound cars on the main road used to be filled with soft-pink carpet roses, but it's recently been concreted. I wait there to cross, noticing that the turning lane is full of fag ends and shards of plastic from the latest car crash. Traffic, up and down. A woman in faded yellow fluoro weaves her mobility scooter across four lanes of cars to reach the other side.

Outside Domino's Pizza a muddy SUV sits with its engine running. The UK's New Weather Institute think tank has called for a ban on advertising for SUVs because the vehicles are jeopardising climate change targets. The institute's report, *Upselling Smoke*, compares SUV advertising to cigarette advertising. A spokesman says, 'In a pandemic-prone world, people need clean air and more space on town and city streets.'[2]

A lowered white car with a noisy exhaust switches to the wrong side of the road without slowing down, taking advantage of the bus stop to avoid the speed bump. Climate change is too far off for most people to worry about.

My bike is the perfect pandemic tool, getting me out of the house and the city, allowing some social contact while staying distanced and helping my lungs recover. It's my escape and my salvation, freeing me from the feeling of being stuck, and from the uncomfortable thought that my real life is going on elsewhere while time trickles through my fingers here.

I like rain and used to commute by bike in all weathers, but since I've been working from home I've let it stop me from cycling. The weather forecast is 'Mostly sunny.' Outside, rain hammers down. By mid-morning the sun is out, so I go for a ride. I've stopped looking down for fungi. Just as well – the roads are busy.

At the city boundary, a new poster says 'Palmy We're Doing Well' above a big yellow heart. A long line of cars, engines idling, queues at the takeaway coffee cart. Rubber donuts are etched on the concrete at the entrance to the river path. Broken alcohol bottles litter the ground. The sun glints off the shards and lights up a meandering silver snail trail – the opposite of boy-racer marks. Someone has stencilled 'CYCLISTS THIS IS NOT A RACETRACK' at intervals all the way along the path. Two young black bulls butt heads in a field.

Two people have been killed and one seriously injured in a car crash in the city. In April, during lockdown, the country had nine road deaths, a record low.

A friend tells me someone threw a full water bottle at her from a car while she was cycling. A purple and yellow bruise spreads across her ribs.

There's frost today, but we've just had the warmest May on record. The garage roof and lawn are covered in white icing. I ride through a large new suburb on the edge of town. As I navigate the roundabout, a man in a black SUV – model name: Raptor – speeds up, squints into the sun and stops suddenly when he sees me. The low sun obscures my visibility and my vision too. Anxiety grips me.

Out I go into the country. Frost lingers in the lee of a tall conifer hedge. It's a still day, and smoke from a distant bonfire flatlines.

Magpies purl and babble in the treetops, and glide overhead. I'm worried they might start divebombing. A broken black bird's wing lies in the grass at the side of the road. I'm uncertain who is the predator and who is the prey.

A middle-aged cyclist in a yellow fluoro jacket is picking up a Coke can from the berm; a large bag of rubbish hangs from his handlebars. It's the man I cleared glass off the road with during lockdown. As I wave to him, a white van passes closely at speed. A couple more speeding cars follow, then the traffic lulls. I count as many bikes as cars and devise a new ritual: the numbers of bikes and cars have to be even to make me feel okay.

Winter solstice, traditionally celebrated in pagan Europe with fire festivals. In te ao Māori, solstice is marked by the turning of the sun god Ra from the sea towards the land.[3] This year it's as warm as summer. At the university, the first daffodils are out, and flower borders brim with brightly coloured anemones. The ginkgo biloba tree hangs on to its golden leaves, its fruit squashed into a baby-sick-scented grey mess on the footpath. Shaggy ink cap mushrooms are still popping up over by the community garden.

It starts raining again just after I get home. Four ducks wheel over the garden against a watery afternoon sky. While picking kale for dinner I spot several sugarsnap pea pods hanging from the plant. This is the way of peas: they seem to appear, suddenly, overnight.

The plants are changing their behaviour, adapting to the changing climate. As we'll have to. But will they, and we, adapt fast enough?

Horizontal rain. Half of the garden is under water. Orange and black recycling bins from the new housing development next door are lined up along the road outside my house. Heather messages to ask if I know what's happening about recycling.

'What do you mean? It's been collected as usual during lockdown.'
'No, it's all been going to landfill.'

When the rain stops, I ride round the airport, past piles of rubbish. Tyre marks form a braided pattern along the road. A red car growls towards me, its engine so loud it's like an aeroplane taking off. At the end of the runway, a bearded young man with brown hair sits in a car, drinking from a flask. A plane spotter. I understand the thrill. For all my claims to be green, I still like the sound of the little planes that come and go from the airport. The noise speaks to me of adventure.

A bird of prey circles. There are slim pickings down here: just litter, most of it takeaway containers. A fabric PAK'nSAVE bag of empty bottles has been dumped on the side of the road. I try to take it as positive that it's not plastic. Nascent watercress grows in the murky brown water in the ditch alongside a berm of dead grass.

Our local Labour MP has been fired following a sex scandal. The election posters of the aberrant MP have been switched out for new ones with a different candidate. 'Let's Keep Moving', says the poster.

The wind is so strong, it blows my helmet back from my forehead. I stop to adjust it and notice plastic orange flowers tied to a street sign. Another death. Further on, plastic bottles, McDonald's wrappers and roadkill – birds, hedgehogs, a rat – are scattered along the shoulder.

At the junction I turn towards town. A peloton of brightly coloured road cyclists is strung out like a chain of paper dolls – riders as far as I can see. A Ranger SUV speeds past; a young man yells out of the passenger window, 'Fuck you! Get the fuck off the road!'

A kingfisher calls from the electricity wire, *Keep going keep going keep going.*

'Winter's arrived,' says the woman at the supermarket checkout. It doesn't feel like winter to me. I'm in a tee-shirt and light rain jacket.

A sign on one side of a café doorway says, 'Chill out – try our new ice chocolate'; on the other side, a sign asks, 'Looking for warm food? Soup and potatoes'. People are as confused as the plants in this crazy weather.

The International Energy Agency warns we only have six months to avert climate crisis. This autonomous agency, created in 1974 in the wake of the oil crisis, says that governments must put money into creating green jobs rather than propping up high-carbon industries with economic recovery plans.[4]

The kids do kapa haka on the school field.

At the lagoon, a greylag goose drinks from a dirty puddle. Two women walk on the path while looking at their phones, oblivious to the cormorant flying in low to land on the water. My victory garden workmate calls this style of walking a phonambulation. I dodge dogs and carry on riding past the army camp towards the prison.

A bus stop is painted with a pastoral scene of a man resting by a river while a boy fishes under his gaze. A little villa sits in the background, and a willow tree drips over the water. Sheep graze under cabbage trees. Flax bloom on the banks. Deer stand below beech trees, and ducks float on the river. I fancy it could be John Batchelar and one of his sons. The remains of glue along the brick-work at the top of the mural look like barbed wire. A plastic yogurt pot and spoon lie on the ground.

On the other side of the road is a drainage ditch. A sign hangs upside down: 'WARNING THIS AREA HAS BEEN SPRAYED. DO NOT COLLECT OR EAT FOOD GATHERED IN THIS AREA'. This end of the ditch is empty, dry, lined with dead grass and weeds, and littered with plastic bottles. Further along, scummy grey water and great clouds of watercress that can't be eaten. Electricity pylons stand at regular intervals. The Defence Force land is separated from the ditch by wooden posts and wire. A small sign says: 'DANGER BIRD SPIKES FITTED'. A blackbird sits on one of the posts anyway.

Back in town, a man is selling watercress from a car parked up at the side of the road. I wonder if the cress was picked from a polluted ditch, and don't stop.

Winter still hasn't arrived. With the neighbour mowing the lawn, and the sun shining, it's almost like a summer's day.

I ride down to the awa (river). The Manawatū Awa dominates the landscape of our region, flowing from the east through the dramatic Manawatū Gorge, wending through the city and on to the sea at Foxton. The awa is a geographical oddity: it's the only one in Aotearoa to cross a mountain range. The Manawatū is older than the mountains through which it flows: the water held its course as the land rose around it, forming the Ruahine and Tararua Ranges.[5]

I continue along the riverbank towards Ashhurst, where a mechanical cutter has hacked back the trees: ragged branch ends resemble splayed toothbrush heads. I skirt around the splinters strewn over the path, then stop to read a sign explaining that the regional council is using willow mulching to control erosion. Mulching, it says, improves vegetation cover, strengthens the trees' roots, and reduces their size, so when the ground is sodden the trees are less likely to fall into the river.

I take off the leggings I'm wearing over my cycle shorts. An older couple walks towards me.

'Going for a swim?' laughs the man.

'You first!' I reply.

You wouldn't want to swim here, I think. In 2009, the river was rated one of the most polluted in the Western world.[6] The resulting outcry led to the creation of the Manawatū River Leaders Forum, which signed an accord to improve the river's mauri (life force) in the hope that it would become a source of regional pride. An information board displays the slogan 'OURS – Manawatū River Leaders' Accord'.

The River Accord website says that in the 1890s Palmerston North installed its first sewage works, which pumped raw sewage into the river. In 1900, after a global bubonic plague scare, the Department of Health ordered that all sewage must be treated. A treatment plant was built five years later. Later still, meatworks and dairy factories were sited on the river so waste could be discharged directly into it. By the 1950s, the river was an open sewer. Agricultural runoff – fertiliser and animal urea – exacerbated the problem. Over the next few decades, large numbers of eels and other fish died from pollution.

The Accord aims to restore the river's health: 'Kei te ora te wai, kei te ora te whenua, kei te ora te tangata / If the water is healthy, the land and the people are nourished.' This is well meaning, but the website says the river 'is precious because it is ours'.[7] That 'ours' bothers me. Why do we think we own the river? And why do we assume that we take precedence over all the other creatures that live here?

In 2017, the Whanganui River was granted its own personhood and described in law as an ancestor of the Whanganui people. This ruling rejects the idea that the awa is the property of humans and recognises that it is its own self.[8] I wish we would do the same here in Manawatū.

The name Manawatū was given to the awa by the early Rangitāne ancestor Hau.[9] Chasing his wife Wairaka, who had eloped with her lover, Hau named each awa he crossed in search of her. On reaching the largest awa of all, Hau's heart (manawa) stood still (tū), both in awe at its beauty and in fear that he wouldn't be able to cross the swiftly flowing water. Hau's courage faltered, but only momentarily. Gathering his resolve, he forged on across the water and continued his journey. When Hau found Wairaka, he turned her into stone.

I cross Fitzherbert Bridge, dodging broken glass, and ride down to the edge of the river, where a large wooden pole records the high-water levels of all major floods of the Manawatū River since written records began. The highest, in 1880, was only a few metres below the top of the stopbank.

I read about the history of flooding in local environmental historian Catherine Knight's book *Ravaged Beauty*. When the city was established in the 1870s, the awa flowed through bush-covered banks. Ten years later, the bush was gone, and the riverside was eroding, particularly around Fitzroy, the area where I live. Early colonists wired willow boughs together and hung them over the bank to take root and stabilise the land. In 1910, Palmerston North Borough Council built a macrocarpa and pine groyne, which is still here, below the bridge. Later, gabions – wood and greywacke stones encased in a wire frame – were placed along the river edge to prevent erosion.

Knight tells the story of Fitzroy resident Mr Snow, who in 1904 asked the council to protect the city from the erosion of land along the edge of the river. But Mr Snow's request was futile, and his house in Fitzroy was eventually washed away.[10]

A friend who lives close by has found an old map of the Fitzroy area. He's going to copy it on to a splashback in his new kitchen. The map shows how the river has moved over time. Since European settlement it has been subject to stopbanking, straightening schemes, sluices and other control measures. The council is still engaged in an endless war with the awa: realigning, draining, dredging it of gravel. But flooding is part of a river's life cycle, its very essence. It flows on, indifferent to us. Occasionally it claims a life. No matter how we try to control it, the awa will continue its own course, wearing down rock and dropping it where it will, breaching its banks, spilling over its floodplains. Climate change will bring more and bigger floods, which will take the bridges and houses and neighbourhoods we've built in the river's path.

Riding home, I pass a cyclist who's stopped on a bridge to look at the stream passing below. A pair of riders on the other side of the road wave to me. A couple more bikes go by, then I see another two up ahead. The bike wheels turn, moving ever onwards, all of us and the river caught up in life's unceasing flow.

It rains and rains. When the showers start to ease off I put on waterproofs and ride to the arboretum. The rain has turned it into a swamp. The Turitea Stream runs fast; along its burst banks, onion weed flows like long green tresses, the hair of a drowned woman.

I creep through a towering bamboo grove and sit below a tree by the stream. Bamboos clack in the wind like kendo swords; I feel as though I'm in a living haiku. I watch the current circle then break free from an eddy, navigating the turbulence to find its way downstream. The water tells me to follow my own course, even when there are obstacles in the way. I sit on the bank and let the water carry away my fears.

# Star

And all the time
the hard stars riding by.

Time, it's a moving stage—
bonfires still blaze
and we hold out our hands
across a widening space

—LAURIS EDMOND, 'Ohakune Fires'[1]

THE MATARIKI STAR CLUSTER rises in the midwinter sky just before
dawn, heralding the start of Māori New Year.
The cluster is approximately one hundred million years old.
Its stars have been significant to humanity through the ages and
across multiple cultures. Waka crews used Matariki to navigate long
distances across the Pacific; ancient Greeks used the same stars,
which they named Pleiades, to explore the Mediterranean. The cluster
even appears in the paintings daubed on a cave wall 17,000 years ago
at Lascaux in France. We'll never know what stories those Paleolithic
artists ascribed to these stars. But Matariki connects us across time
and space, helps us find our way across the planet, and guides us
through the seasons of our lives.

Māori New Year starts at the same time in the natural cycle as the
new year does in the northern hemisphere, a few weeks after winter
solstice. Europeans imposed an alien calendar here, disregarding
Aotearoa's seasonal alignment, in an early form of globalisation
that ignored local differences. This sparks the thought that Matariki
highlights the similarities between the indigenous culture in Aotearoa
and my own ancient culture in the north, before the natural world

was decreed irrelevant by industrialisation. Despite our modern lives, we're all connected by the same complex web of life.

Matariki is an important time in the cycle of food growing and gathering. The stars appear soon after harvest, when pātaka are well stocked with supplies for the coming year. The arrival of Matariki signals that the calendar has come full circle, and the season to plant is here again. It's time to celebrate new life and think about the future.[2]

But Matariki also serves as a time to remember and grieve for those who have died since the cluster last appeared, and whose spirits have become stars. This is reflected in the whakatauki:

> *Haere atu rā e koro ki te paepae o Matariki. O Rehua.*
> *Haere atu rā.*
> *Farewell old man, go to the threshold of Matariki. Of Rehua.*
> *Farewell.*[3]

A colleague rings to tell me that one of our work friends has terminal cancer and has only days to live. She's making a dash across the country to see her in the hospice before she dies. I give her a farewell message to deliver, knowing I won't see my friend again: she's too sick for more visitors.

It's a cold day. I head to the arboretum, where I always go when I feel sad. A rainbow lorikeet flies squawking through the trees, a streak of primary colours. A blackbird bursts out of a bush, scattering raindrops. The lemony smell of wintersweet wafts from an invisible bush. The Turitea Stream gurgles, and a large leaf floats down from a giant nashi pear tree. I spot a couple of dog-walkers, and turn the other way.

Back towards home, a sign at the city boundary says: 'ARMAGEDDON. EXPERIENCE THE INCREDIBLE'. It promises 'Armageddon is back, just not the one you were expecting!' A fictional Armageddon postponed – because a real one seemed more likely.

That night as I eat dinner, the lights go out. I feel momentarily freaked out, and scramble around for candles. Almost an hour later it gets cold, so I go walking. Better than sitting at home freezing, and anyway I quite like the dark. Maybe it's the Orcadian-Norse ancestry I get from Nana. I aim for the streetlights a block further on, but just as I get there, they switch off too. An indistinct human shape walks down a driveway, and I feel uneasy. Maybe I should head home. I turn around, then hear a female voice say, 'Evening'.

Relief.

A cyclist in a long black anorak, Covid mask concealing his face, comes swooping around the corner, rides along the footpath, no lights, no helmet, pulls out into traffic and sits in the middle of the road waiting for a gap, almost invisible. His hood and flapping coat make him look like the Grim Reaper, and I wonder if he has a death wish.

The air smells of rain and smoke. Safely home, the lights come on, and I make a cup of tea and huddle over the heater. A cacophony of sirens outside. It feels like the end of days.

Another cold, wet day. Rain drips from the boughs of the plum tree. I'm waiting for news of my sick friend. I think I hear a message drop on the computer, but it's a bird in the garden uttering a single forlorn note.

I can't focus on work, don't want to be inside. I go out and walk round and round and round the field, shivering as the cold wind and rain batter my face.

Four o'clock on a random Friday. Our friend is gone. Grief comes in waves. I look at the little hill in my garden where I stood talking to her on the phone just a few weeks ago. She'd told me she hadn't left the house since lockdown started but had made no mention of her illness. I'd tried to encourage her to go walking.

I head out to the field; I'm anxious to see the sunset. I'm afraid that, if I miss it, I might not get another one. People drive home from work, looking forward to the weekend. Life continues. The world rushes resolutely on.

The week passes in a blur. Four of us drive to Hawke's Bay in pouring rain for our friend's funeral. She was famous for her social justice work; well-known faces deliver eulogies. In life, she sparkled. We decorate her coffin with shiny confetti and write goodbye messages with glitter pens.

Farewell, dear friend. Haere atu rā.

I walk to the hospital for routine blood tests. Past the Salt Therapy Centre: 'Breathe Better Live Better', says the sign. The usual gaggle of smokers stands outside the hospital; cigarette butts litter the ground. A hearse pulls into the Church of St Mary next door to the shiny new birthing centre. A statue of the Virgin looks down on the vehicle as it pulls up with its cargo of a flower-topped coffin.

Minus two degrees overnight, frost on the garden. Is this winter at last? But how can it be winter when there are still tiny yellow and white buds on the rose bushes, and pink blossoms appearing out of dark branches on the ornamental plum tree by the gate?

Someone has stuck a handwritten sign on the pātaka kai: 'Don't be greedy. This is for everyone.' The pātaka kai contains three large bags of lemons and two boxes of empty jam jars. I take some of each. If life gives you lemons and jam jars, make lemon curd.

I made winter bird feeders a couple of days ago: molten Kremelta, mixed with wild bird seed, packed into cups with string tied to the handles. When the fat set, I hung them in the plum tree. It's taken a couple of days for the birds to figure them out, but today there are loads of birds on the feeders. The waxeyes are acrobats, hanging upside down from twigs to get to the food. The greenfinches are less agile and can't seem to reach the fat. But after half a day they've worked out that they can land on the feeder itself and cling on to the rim while pecking at the food. One greenfinch seems dominant. He's a bit of a bully: he hogs the feeder, pecking at birds that come near, or rearing up and flapping his wings at them. Occasionally he'll tolerate another bird eating at the same time. Tūī have migrated to the front of the house to feed on the pink ornamental-plum blossom. One of them breaks off feasting on the blooms to come and take a look; he seems incongruously large next to the other birds. Sparrows hop around underneath, picking up the dropped seeds. Blackbirds squabble. Don't fight, I think, there's enough for everybody.

Work is busy. When I finally switch off the computer at 5.30, I rush out to the field for my walk, worried that I've missed the sunset, but the sun is still going down, and the whole sky is fuchsia, orange and gold. I can't drag my eyes away from the light. As I turn around the apex of the track, I see the huge, bright full moon in the dark-pink sky above the ranges. I feel insignificant but connected. We're so inconsequential with our petty quarrels.

'Dwell on the beauty of life. Watch the stars, and see yourself running with them,' said Marcus Aurelius, Roman emperor and philosopher.

I lie on the back deck in a big coat and stare out into space. British Astronomer Royal Martin Rees says that we're all made of atoms created when stars were formed. Everything on this planet exists because of stars, he says: light and heat from the biggest star of all – the sun – give us life; the very substances of which we're composed were forged in the heavens. We are stardust, every one of us, born in the same stars, ancient and far away.[4]

We're lucky here, in our semi-rural environment, because stars are visible on clear nights. In many places, the stars are blotted out by artificial luminescence. During lockdown, some city-dwellers saw stars for the first time.

It's extraordinary to think that all the people who have ever existed lived under the same sky and the same constellations. We may have differently interpreted the patterns in that sky, or their meanings, but they're common to every human society that has ever been, and possibly will ever be. Stargazing is humbling: it requires us to adjust our sense of importance downwards, and it puts our problems into perspective. Rees points out that when we consider star time, it doesn't seem credible that humans represent the end point of the evolutionary process. The stars pre-exist us and will probably outlive us too. But even stars die eventually. The light from dead stars continues to shine but is eventually absorbed into the darkness.

I'm at the optometrist for a check-up. She's slightly worried about something she sees in my eyes and sends me for a glaucoma test. Glaucoma is a disease of the optic nerve that starts at the outer edge of the eye; peripheral vision is the first thing to disappear. I sit in a darkened room, looking into a large metal box, clicking a button every time I see a dot of light. *Click click click.* I score 100 percent, though I tell the operator I wasn't sure if I'd imagined some of the lights. He tells me that we have a blind spot where our optic nerve connects to the retina, but our brain fills in the missing part of the picture. I ask if this is why stars disappear when I look directly at them. He explains that our eyes have rods, which work in low light, and cones, which work in bright light. When we look at objects at night, we detect them with the rods. The rods are concentrated in the corners of our eyes, so when we look at the stars, we see them more clearly if we look slightly to the side.

When you search for the past, or the truth, it often slips away. But sometimes when you're looking in another direction, it strays into your vision.

I'm lying in my bottom bunk in the teenage bedroom I share with my sisters. Someone is shaking me.

'Wake up,' says my elder sister. 'Something's happened.' I open my eyes and look at her. 'Dad's died.'

Mum appears in the doorway; she walks to the bed, and I throw my arms around her. No warning. No farewell messages. The rest is a blur.

Like me, Dad was seventeen when his father died of heart failure. Two years earlier, in 1944, he had lost his eldest brother to the Luftwaffe on a bombing raid over Germany. The Royal Air Force motto: Per ardua ad astra (Through adversity to the stars). After the war, Dad followed his brother's footsteps into the RAF for his national service as an aircraft mechanic. Shortly after leaving the air force in 1958, he met Mum at a dance. He emerged from the toilets, spotted Mum, and crossed the hall towards her.

'Would you like to dance?'

'All right.'

Dad took his cigarette out of his mouth, dropped it on the wooden floor and ground it under his shoe. Then they were off. Mum says Dad was a lovely dancer. They kept dancing for many years after we were born, Mum in a glitzy orange and copper dress that caught the light and threw out spangles as she spun. I still have that dress, although it's far too tiny for me to fit into.

There were no more dances for my parents after we moved to the council estate. Dad did early shifts. My elder sister was the one going out dancing now. I became a sullen, introverted teenager and had drifted away from Dad by the time he died. There are so many questions I would ask him now. And I'm just beginning to understand his life in a way I never could have done at seventeen.

I have a silk portrait of Dad in his RAF uniform, painted in Japan in 1949. We found it after his bachelor brother moved into a retirement villa in the late 1990s. The portrait was folded up in the attic of the council house that had been the family home. I wondered why the picture hadn't been on display, but maybe my grandmother didn't want to remember the war.

Dad never met any of his five grandchildren. My nephew who recently turned nineteen looks just like Dad did at the same age. He's studying aeronautical engineering at technical college, following in his unknown grandad's footsteps.

Per ardua ad astra, Dad.

The house across from me has a huge chandelier hanging in its upstairs window. The people living there leave it on all night. Its light beams directly into my bedroom through a gap at the edge of the blind and bounces off the mirror into my eyes when I'm in bed. Today I move the mirror to a different wall and hang curtains over the blind.

Humans have always tried to defeat the darkness. First with fire, as soon as our ancestors learnt to control it. The earliest lamps were made from shells and hollow rocks filled with moss and animal fat. These have been found in the Lascaux caves and were perhaps used by those early artists when painting the stars on the cave walls. Later came rushlights and candles, then lamps of terracotta, glass and metal, fuelled by plant and animal oils and beeswax. Gas and coal-fired lights became common in towns from the early nineteenth century.[5] The novelist Robert Louis Stevenson wrote that, with the coming of gaslight, city dwellers had 'stars of their own; biddable domesticated stars'.[6] Drilling for petroleum for oil lamps started in 1859. Then came electricity. In 1881 my hometown of Godalming in

Surrey became the first place in the world to have a public electricity supply. The streetlights were a tourist attraction; one Christmas my brother sent me an old postcard showing the town lit up by the novel electric light. In the early 1900s, neon signs appeared. In the Western world, the mystery of night had disappeared.[7]

In 1921, Katherine Mansfield wrote to her cousin, the Countess Russell, of sitting on a balcony in Switzerland when 'it's too dark to write or to do anything but wait for the stars … sitting like a shadow at the door of one's being while the dark tide rises … It is so easy to forget, in a worldly life, to attend to these miracles.'[8]

We might be addicted to artificial light, but other species are damaged by it. I read an article by British naturalist Matt Gaw in *Resurgence and Ecologist*. Gaw writes about how our illumination of the darkness affects plants, fish, birds, mammals, reptiles, amphibians and, most of all, insects, interrupting migration, hunting, mating and breeding. Insects are dying of sheer exhaustion under what Gaw calls 'the searchlights of the Anthropocene'. There's a simple solution, he says: turn the lights off.[9]

Biking along the awa after dark, I ride up onto He Ara Kotahi bridge through the new star path, a section of the track that's lit up with luminous spheres set into the ground. I wonder about the effect of this light on the creatures that live along here. I've read on the council website that the path uses no energy and emits no light pollution – 'people with homes near the river won't be disturbed' – but it doesn't mention other species.[10] Still, this seems like a good solution for the problem of needing to see our way home in the dark while not polluting the night sky.

The website says there's a new artwork on its way for the river path, using the same illumination technique. The design, by Rangitāne tohunga whakairo Warren Warbrick, is inspired by the whakatauki about the growth of the Rangitāne people:[11]

*Tini whetū ki te rangi*
*Ko Tānenui-a-rangi ki te whenua.*
*Like the multitude of stars in the sky*
*So great is Rangitāne on the earth.*[12]

Riding home, I watch the stars come out one by one: the darkness bringing forth light.

Starbursts of white flowers appear on the plum tree. A thrush tugs at strands of alyssum in the flower border below the trellis, searching for material for its nest. New life is coming.

My workmates and I host a farewell lunch for a colleague who's having a baby. We buy her a blueberry bush so the child can pick her own fruit when she's big enough. My colleague with the victory garden brings a beautiful salad of purple beetroot, Chinese and red cabbages, and orange marigold petals.

'Victory cabbages!' he says.

As I ride home, the wind drives cold, hard rain into my face, pricking my skin, but the pain is invigorating, like tiny acupuncture needles.

I've been neglecting the garden over winter, caught up in my grief. I put my bike in the garage and instead of going straight into the warmth of the house I search through the seed tin and find half a packet of rainbow mix heritage tomatoes. I fill trays with seed-raising mix and sow the tomatoes, then bring them inside to germinate in the airing cupboard.

At night the sound of the freight train carried on the wind wakes me. I look out of the window at the stars and feel grateful to be alive.

# Stone

**MY TRAMPING BUDDY** and I go to walk in Te Āpiti, the Manawatū Gorge. The gorge divides the Tararua and Ruahine mountain ranges that border Manawatū. The ranges, composed of greywacke stone covered with marine sediments, were formed about three million years ago and uplifted over the past million. This sounds ancient, but they're the youngest mountain ranges in the world. The native podocarps – trees with cones and berries – and nīkau palms that cover the gorge like a cloak give a glimpse of what this region was like before the forest fell to fire and axe.

George Petersen's 1952 book *The Pioneering Days of Palmerston North* includes a description of the gorge written by an English visitor in 1885. The tourist talks of masses of giant tōtara covered in lichen, moss and creepers, howling wind, furious water, mists, cliffs and crags, forming a picture of 'inexpressible beauty and indescribable grandeur'.[2]

Today the gorge is busy, with lots of families milling around. The road through Te Apiti, hewn from the rock in 1872 to connect east and west, has been closed since 2017 after a series of landslips made it too expensive and time-consuming to maintain. A new state highway is planned to carry traffic east across the ranges. The old gorge road now stops at the car park. There the tarmac is covered in black rubber donuts; large concrete barriers stop the joyriders going further. Beyond this point, the road is deep in gravel. A big pile of fly-tipped electronics and household rubbish sits nearby. Two men in hoodies, with bulldogs straining on leads, walk up the road with a pair of small boys who clamber over the concrete barriers.

'I thought dogs weren't allowed,' my friend says.

Dogs aren't allowed, but I'm not going to say anything to the men.

We pass through an area of interpretation boards, walk under the road bridge and enter the bush on the other side. It's cool, dark and green; a stream gurgles downhill. It's quiet, very quiet. There's no car noise up here. But the silence is disconcerting.

'I can't hear any birds,' says my friend. A bit further on she pauses, listens; a riroriro/grey warbler sings, and a tūī calls. These two birds are all we hear. Instead of live birds, there are wooden posts bearing plasticised pictures of different species, and a QR code to scan so you can hear what a real bird would sound like if it were here and singing.

After a steep walk uphill, we stop at a lookout and sit on a bench eating sandwiches as we gaze over Manawatū, across the fields, to the road in the distance with its tiny cars. We're both migrants from Europe; we talk about homesickness; how much we miss our families on the other side of the world; wonder when we'll see them again. She starts to cry. I take her hand and tell her everything is going to be okay. I'm trying to convince myself, too.

A family appears at the lookout, so we say hi, then pack our bags and keep walking to a clearing further up, where a sculpture of the great twelfth-century Māori explorer Whātonga looms from the trees above us. The sign tells us that Whātonga sailed from his home in Heretaunga (present-day Hawke's Bay), around the coast and inland along the Manawatū Awa. When he came to the gorge, he looked

down on huge forests and plentiful food sources, including tuna
(eels), kererū, kākā, kākāpō, kiore and berries. He named the region
Te Tapere Nui o Whātonga (the food basket of Whātonga). Later,
he came back with his people and settled the area: his descendants
are the Rangitāne iwi of Manawatū. The sculpture features intricate
pattern work depicting aspects of Whātonga's world: a kōwhaiwhai
pattern called mangōpare (hammerhead shark), reflecting the
explorer's sea voyages, and an egg shape called ngutu kākā, depicting
the wild fowl harvested by Rangitāne.[3]

From the next lookout, we see far below us Te Au Rere a Te Tonga
(the rushing current of the south)/White Horse Rapids, up which
Māori hauled their waka when travelling from the east. A huge rust-
coloured rock called Te Ahu a Tūranga sits in the river. Legend says
that this rock is never submerged, and that it holds the mauri of the
awa and of the Rangitāne iwi.[4]

My friend drops me back home.

'Kia kaha,' I tell her. 'Stay strong.'


When we say that something is set in stone, we mean it's immutable,
permanent. But stone wears down over time, crumbles in the weather,
is consumed by lichen. Stone is always changing; it just happens at
a rate beyond human timeframes. Stone, then, holds two seemingly
opposed concepts: permanence and transfiguration.

I ride past the gravel pit on the far side of the city. The river gravel
that underlies Palmerston North has been used to construct railways
and roads since the city's early days. Our need to keep moving has
transformed this area.

Along the river path, white toetoe echo the shape of black flax
flowers. The white cat that appears on the ranges when snow settles
is clearly visible. Winter lays bare the skeleton of the landscape;
the ranges form the region's backbone. I stop at a clearing and sit

on a gabion that's been made into a seat. Three people on gravel motorbikes rev their engines down by the water.

On the way home, I ride past a man who's moving big greywacke boulders into a vast decorative pile at the end of a driveway.

'That's a big job!' I call.

'She certainly is,' he says.

A small hedgehog snuffles about by the gutter on my street. It shouldn't be out in daylight; I wonder if it's sick. I know they are pests here, but hedgehogs are endangered in Britain, and I was brought up on Beatrix Potter's tales of Mrs Tiggywinkle. I can't bring myself to kill them. I don't have any patience with the depiction of any creature as evil – this is anthropomorphism as much as Beatrix Potter's tales are. The ancestors of these animals were brought here to serve a function for humans, and they've caused drastic imbalances in the ecosystem.

Introduced animals need to be controlled if we want to protect indigenous flora and fauna. But I can't help thinking that we've wiped out or endangered many of the native species of Aotearoa ourselves, and rather than curtailing our actions we seek a scapegoat. From the comfort of our homes and cars and supermarkets we don't see that the hedgehogs, and every other species, must compete for food and shelter in the increasingly small space left unoccupied by humans.

I ask a man clearing an abandoned section if a new housing development is going in. No, he says, he's just clearing it on behalf of the owner, using poison on the noxious weeds, by order of the council. He rolls his eyes, then tells me he's been in the Ruahines shooting deer; he lived in the bush for three days before coming out to 'this madness'. He says that people sometimes say hunting isn't okay, but he reckons supermarket culture isn't okay. Then he shows me photos on his phone: fish, decapitated deer, his grandchildren.

I steer the conversation away from the grandkids by telling him that what's considered a pest here is often an endangered species in the UK. I'm still thinking about the hedgehog.

'We don't like successful species,' I say.

'Like rats,' he says.

We talk about the unusual old Spanish-style house on the section; it's been empty for the eight years I've lived here. Then we get on to the subject of the old villa that was recently removed from the end of the street, along with its rose gardens and native trees, replaced by a subdivision of new-builds, with concrete slabs and pebbles where plants once grew. He rolls his eyes again.

'You're English, aren't you?' he says. He tells me he likes old things, and that his English ancestors were diamond merchants who are buried in Tewkesbury Abbey: 'Ten generations. There's a stone in the floor.'

Mum has paid an undertaker to reinscribe Dad's gravestone, worn down by time. It cost a fortune but, she says, 'It's one last thing I can do for him.'

The undertaker is an old schoolmate of mine. Flashback to secondary school careers class, 1981. We all had to say what we wanted to be when we grew up. We went around the room: musician, accountant, footballer, mechanic, farmer, pilot, book editor (me). Then a boy said, 'Undertaker.' The other kids laughed.

The teacher shushed us and asked, 'Why do you want to be an undertaker?'

'Well, people are always going to die, so I'll never be out of a job,' he said.

Two years later I started sixth form at the college in town. This used to be the local grammar school; Mum went there in the early 1950s and still has books that she won for academic excellence.

Sixth form was a different world from the village secondary school. Latin class: the teacher was late, and a tall blond boy was determining rank.

'Okay, tell me what your father does,' he said in a posh voice.

We went around the room: TV producer, barrister, doctor, professor, postman (me). He looked at me, paused and gave a brief nod. I had no idea what it meant. It's trendy now to wear your working-class status on your sleeve, but it wasn't then. My new friends lived in houses with names – Wentworth Grange, Bramley House – but council houses only had numbers. We'd moved from Avon Cottage, backing on to a common, to 64 Oak Mead, slap bang in town where there were very few oaks still in evidence. Mum remembers the area before the council estate was built, after the war; standing on the hill above what's now housing, she says, you could look out for miles over woodlands.

Three days after Dad died, I took my Cambridge University entrance exam. A handful of us sat at desks in a silent room, then the teacher said, 'You may begin.' I opened the exam paper and one question jumped out at me: 'Explore themes of death and dying in twentieth-century literature.' I scanned the rest of the questions. I couldn't answer any of them. I stood up and left the room.

My English teacher came after me, looking concerned. 'What happened?'

I burst into tears, and when I told him, he looked as if he wanted to cry too.

Back home, Mum said, 'I think it's a good thing you don't go to Cambridge. The people might be snooty, and you wouldn't fit in.'

I went to university in Norwich, an ancient city of old stone houses, pubs and a castle, centred around a limestone, flint and mortar cathedral. The cathedral has been repeatedly damaged by lightning, wind, fire and riots, but it endures. The cathedral's stone bosses, high up in the ceiling vaults, are some of the world's greatest

Medieval sculptures, depicting flowers and leaves, pagan green men and scenes of the apocalypse.

I walk to the old cemetery a couple of kilometres from my house. I've been meaning to explore this place for ages but never seemed to find the time. But now time spreads out before me.

The city's first cemetery was located in a swampy area of town, but when bodies started to rise to the surface – the dead rejoining the living – the cemetery was relocated to Napier Road. The old site is now home to the speedway.

In the old cemetery the early history of the city is spelt out in stone. About ten thousand people were interred between 1872 and 1927. The online guidebook notes that many colonists were killed clearing the dense tōtara and kahikatea bush surrounding the settlement. These were hard times. In the 1870s, 10 percent of children died before their first birthdays from illnesses such as croup, pneumonia, tuberculosis, whooping cough or diphtheria – illnesses that today can be prevented or treated by vaccines and antibiotics. Stillborn babies were buried in their own area.

But there was wealth in the young city too. An ornate mausoleum houses the remains of the Wilson family, the first in Palmerston North to own a car (an Oldsmobile, for the record). The Nashes are buried here too: Norman, the owner of the *Manawatu Evening Standard*, and James Alfred, mayor and MP for Palmerston North, namesake of my street, and the man who built the grand villa that used to sit on the terrace above my house.

The multicultural society that was early Palmerston North is writ large in the cemetery. The oldest Māori headstone is dated 10 May 1888 and commemorates Meritini Te Panau of the Rangitāne Te Awe Awe whānau. Her husband Kerei, who lived to about 103 years old, is also buried here.

At this time Palmerston North had a small Chinese community, many of whom were market gardeners. One of these was Ah-Yung, who died in 1884. The local newspaper reported that his countrymen were upset at Ah-Yung's dying in a strange land. Chinese residents travelled to the cemetery annually, leaving fruit, rice, nuts and sweets as food for the dead. They also left flowers – sustenance for the soul, perhaps – and let off firecrackers.

Catholics are buried in the same small patch as Presbyterians, Anglicans, Jews, Wesleyans and Lutherans; Māori, Irish, British, Chinese and Scandinavians lie side by side; OBEs and VCs rub shoulders with 'ordinary' citizens and soldiers. One of those soldiers had returned from the trenches of World War I only to die of the Spanish flu that swept the globe after the war. In November 1918, All Saints Anglican Church alone buried sixty flu victims in twenty days; they would normally bury eight people in that period. The influenza epidemic put such a strain on the cemetery that a new one was built in 1927 at Kelvin Grove, named for an area of Glasgow in Scotland. In New Zealand, from a population of one million, more than 6700 people died of Spanish flu. Scaled up to today's population, that would be about 32,000 deaths.

In 1902, the *Manawatu Evening Standard* complained that 'cyclists are … in the habit of riding through the cemetery on their machines'. The Cemetery Committee vowed to deal with such 'objectionable practices'.[5] As I stand pondering the war graves, I hear a motor. A large young man in jandals, shorts and tee-shirt astride a tiny dirt bike heads straight towards me along the narrow path of the cemetery. I back up against the bank, catching his eye as he rides past, but he makes no acknowledgement. Plus ça change.

The cemetery houses the remains of the long-dead, but also serves as a place of remembrance for the living. Memories reside in teddy bears sculpted on a child's grave; stones left on a Jewish tomb;

narratives of deaths by house fires or murders. Loss and grief are encoded here in stone. But there's also an area of the cemetery that has no physical memorials, because those who lie here had no money for such things. Names and events etched on stone tell only part of the story of a life, or a place, just as history books do. The rest lives in memory, in the landscape, in the gaps.

The cemetery links the past to the present and connects us to the future. I look out across the stones, over the road, up to the distant hills. Crisp brown leaves float down from the trees, get picked up by a light breeze, and are blown away from Palmerston North.

I walk to Memorial Park, where an interpretation board gives the site's history. This area used to be a gravel pit, providing ballast for the region's railways, but as trains got heavier the Railways Department switched to crushed rock, and the pit became obsolete by the time of World War II. The city was left with a huge hole in the ground, which the council bought in 1938 to create Fitzroy Park. In 1952, a pink marble obelisk war memorial was installed, and two years later the area was renamed Fitzroy Memorial Park. (The city's official war memorial, where the names of the fallen are inscribed, stands in Te Marae o Hine/The Square.) But the memorial was neglected, and slowly crumbled away before being removed in 1983. A small plaque commemorating women who served in the forces in World War II is still here.

In 2011, the park became a workers' memorial in honour of twenty-two-year-old Irishman John Kelly, who died in the city brickworks in 1904 when under-strength scaffolding collapsed. Kelly's employer, Ike Fake, was found not guilty of negligence but left Palmerston North soon after Kelly's funeral. Before he went, he bought an extravagant mausoleum for Kelly in the old cemetery. And so a penniless ditch digger ended up in a bigger vault than the mayor's, and lies beneath the only stone in the cemetery to show a portrait of the deceased.[6]

More people die at work than in wars. A memorial plaque on a big chunk of rock at the park entrance is inscribed: 'If blood be the price of your cursed wealth – then truly we have bought it fair'. The words are based on a poem called 'We Have Fed You All for a Thousand Years' written by 'an unknown proletariat'.[7] A smaller plaque remembers another Kelly, union leader Helen, who died of cancer in 2016, aged fifty-two.

Like everywhere, Manawatū is a palimpsest, with layers of texts and meanings. This place has been created by previous interactions between people, creatures and landscape. Its memorials speak of some of the people who came to the region, and the lives they spent here: wealthy or destitute, quiet or eventful, short or long.

The lives of our ancestors progressed at a slow pace. Some stayed in one place, perhaps a single village, their whole lives. Those who moved did so slowly, by waka, sailing ship, horse or their own feet. But we live in a state of perpetual, rapid motion, and it's addictive. I've been still for too long, and I'm feeling homesick again. The walls of the room feel too close; the possibility of not being able to leave here is unendurable.

I go out for a ride through one of the rapidly expanding city suburbs. It feels like senior citizen country: retirement village, bungalows, campervans, garden statuary. A grinning gnome in a red hat stands alongside a Roman emperor. An old blue villa, forlorn, for sale, has been crowded out by the cemetery on one side and the housing development that moves like a wave of magma outwards from the city on the other. Poised between life and death, its time is marked. I ride past a new road sign: 'Freedom Drive. No exit'. I feel as though I'm waiting to die in Palmerston North, and this fills me with mild panic.

A flock of pigeons flies up, reflecting silver light from grey and white feathers, matching the roofs and walls of the new houses. As I turn the corner, I catch the wind and take off, away from the suburbs.

A green furze of new crops covers the fields in the market gardens. Lambs already, and tiny white dots of blossom on wilding plum trees. Starlings glisten green and blue on an apple tree; the yellow fruit glows like tiny golden baubles among the bare branches. I stop to take off a layer and eat biscuits. The sun is hot on my legs. Cows move methodically along the berm, mowing the grass, jostling for the fresh green growth. A pīwakawaka darts around them, comes over to check me out. Two daffodils bloom in the grass.

We memorialise negative events in stone: wars, disasters, deaths. But Palmerston North has plenty of sculptures and statues relating to good things too: tangata whenua and settlers from all lands; birds, trees, flowers, animals; peace and diversity.

I have an appointment in town. I get there early and sit gathering my thoughts on a concrete wall in Te Marae o Hine, near the statue of Rangitāne leader and tipuna Te Peeti Te Awe Awe.

A little boy in gumboots climbs on a rock carving near me.

He looks at me and says, 'I'm good at climbing eh?'

'You are! That's awesome.'

A girl, with a smaller child on her back, calls him.

'You'd better go,' I say, but the boy doesn't move.

The girl comes over, hoists the child further up her back.

'Come on bubba.'

The boy clambers down awkwardly and the three of them leave.

The sculpture is a chunky circle of rock with a hole in the middle. In Southwest England, where Dad's family lived for generations, the story goes that if you pass through a hole in a large stone you move into a new phase of life. The hole is too small for me to fit, but I put my hand through it and hope that will be enough.

# Spring

Blossom—Bird—Wind

# Blossom

Kia puta mai tou whanau,
Tipu ake, hei putiputi pauwai
Mo tea o whanui.

May your family grow,
and emerge, like flowers blooming
over the wider world.

—ARAPERA HINEIRA KAA BLANK, 'To a Sensitive Person'[1]

**TODAY IS OFFICIALLY THE FIRST DAY OF SPRING.** As I open the airing cupboard to get a towel, I notice that the tomato seeds have germinated. Delicate, pale seedlings emerge from the soil, like hope in a pot. I move the plants to a sunny spot on the windowsill then go into the garden. A solitary lipstick-pink tulip blooms at the appointed time.

Over winter I lost momentum through a combination of lingering illness, ennui, loneliness, and rain that felt endless. On this bright spring morning, newborn monarch butterflies blaze black and burnt-orange against pure white plum blossom, and my spirits rise with them.

Spring begins with its customary bluster. Blossom falls from the plum tree like a shower of confetti. I pick grapefruit for breakfast and sugarsnap peas for dinner, then rescue a bunch of fragrant narcissi that are being buffeted by wind and rain. The flowers bring cheer to the house.

On the way into town to get library books, I pass the Covid testing station where three women in PPE stand talking on the footpath, without customers. In the UK, Covid-19 cases – and deaths – are rising. Family and friends there face restrictions again as they head into winter, while our world reawakens.

We may be urbanised now, and removed from the seasonality of the natural world, but even in the city signs of spring are evident as we tilt back towards the sun. Waxy, white magnolia flowers open like candelabra against bare branches, scenting the air with lemon and honey. Around the edges of Te Marae o Hine, purple, orange and white pansies march in orderly rows.

Two days of cold and wet. But a tinge of green appears on the trees on the field as the world quickens. Creamy blossoms dot the elder, pumping out their cat-pee scent; catkins dangle from hazels and birches; and clusters of butter-yellow flowers hang from dark brown kōwhai branches. Kōwhai is Aotearoa New Zealand's national flower; in te ao Māori, its arrival heralds spring.[2]

If I'm going to reduce my supermarket dependence, I need to make my own booze, so I pick elderflowers for champagne. I put the flowers in a bucket with sugar, lemons and boiled water, and set them aside to ferment. I make cordial too, four bottles, for summer drinks.

Elder is sometimes known as witches' tree. In English and Scandinavian folklore, the tree's spirit is the elder mother, a pre-Christian vegetation goddess. It's said that if an elder grows in your garden, she's chosen to protect you.[3]

A couple of years after Dad died, when my younger sister finished school, Mum went to work at the British Embassy in Tokyo. She'd never been abroad before, but after leaving school at fourteen, marrying five years later, having four children, and working for most of her life in our hometown, this was her chance to blossom. Funny that she ended up in Japan, as Dad had done during his National

Service almost forty years earlier. Both of them flying away and landing in the same place. The silk portrait of Dad depicts a miniature Mount Fuji, surrounded by sakura trees in blossom. It was painted just before his twenty-first birthday. I went to Japan for the first time just before my twenty-first too; in fact, I spent my birthday in the air, being fussed over by flight attendants.

Mum became quite a traveller after Tokyo, visiting Italy, Norway, the USA, Bangladesh (to visit my brother, who worked there). She even did a world tour on a cargo boat, stopping at New Zealand on the way, long before I came here. Right then I was getting to know the Kiwi with whom I emigrated two years later. Mum came to Aotearoa once more, in 2010, just after that relationship ended. My younger sister later told me that Mum had come here to look after me.

Fitzroy is a haze of pastel cherry blossom. A man hangs bubblegum-pink and pale-yellow balloons on a gate for a party. A few blocks away, developers have pulled down an old villa and builders are constructing new homes in its place. I'm distracted by a garden where lilac wisteria climbs up a wooden pillar with a flare of yellow flowers at its base. I peer around the fence – the yellow flowers are oxalis. Another joyous cluster of the same plant decorates a patch of grass on the berm around a tree trunk.

The vegetable bed, with its vivid, clashing colours, is a Fauvist canvas: magenta flowers unfurl on the broad beans, kale bursts into yellow florets, and marigolds sport orange petals. There's a strong wind forecast, so I tie the bean plants to bamboo stakes to protect them.

At the back edge of the garden, I kneel to drink in the powdery, intoxicating scent from a carpet of pale-mauve violets.

Later, the sky darkens as a storm approaches. I love the sheer drama of it: the sense of apprehension when the lights are lowered;

the threat of impending disaster as the tempest nears; the fear as the thunder booms and the lightning flashes; then the rain, the main player. Catharsis as the sun reappears and a chorus of birds sings.

They need rain in California. The state is on fire.

'It'll start getting cooler, you just watch,' says US President Donald Trump as he visits the area. He adds that he thinks science doesn't know about global warming.[4]

Australia is also in flames. Australian environmental scientist Tim Flannery, writing in the *Guardian*, draws a parallel between coronavirus and carbon monoxide, both travelling invisibly through the air, threatening our civilisation. Flannery points out that while the Australian government takes drastic action to stop Covid-19, it does nothing to prevent the accumulation of carbon monoxide as the burning of fossil fuels increases global temperatures, causing the floods, droughts and fires that plague the country. He gives a terrible statistic: in summer 2019–20, more than 21 percent of Australia's forests were on fire.[5]

Here, the winter of 2020 was the warmest on record, and spring is going in the same direction. New Zealand environmental scientist George Perry tells the *Guardian* that we're heading towards a more flammable landscape as the planet heats up. He says that most New Zealanders are ready for earthquakes, tsunamis and volcanic eruptions but haven't thought about the threat from fire.[6]

We weren't prepared for a pandemic either. Viruses and megafires raging across the globe – is this what the end of the world looks like? Or do we dare hope that fire might also mean rebirth?

Māori legend tells how the fire goddess Mahuika set the forest ablaze after being deceived by the trickster Māui, who'd tried to steal her magic. In terror of being burnt alive in the furnace that raged around him, Māui appealed for help to his ancestor Tāwhirimātea, god of wind and storms. Tāwhirimātea sent a flood to extinguish the flames and save Māui's life. But the water could not destroy Mahuika. She threw the seeds of fire high into the māhoe and kaikōmako trees, in whose wood the gift of fire is retained.[7]

Rising early, the world is fresh and young. From the Linton bike path there's a crystal-clear view of the mountain, a frosting of snow on the southern ranges. Young calves wear coats against the cold, and tiny lambs gambol on wobbly legs in a swampy field, delighted with their new lives on this shining spring day.

On campus, Mr Bull's rhododendrons and azaleas are a mishmash of clashing colours: pink, white, orange, mauve, red. Bees clamber inside blooms to collect pollen. Students take selfies under an avenue of Japanese flowering cherries. The Japanese know that sakura teaches us to appreciate the beauty of the moment, because all too soon it will be gone. Despite this bittersweet metaphor, it's hard to grasp how brief our existence is against the endlessness of eternity. This thought makes me want to seize life with a new intensity.

Nine tūī bob about in a tall, slender cherry tree; they are difficult to count because they constantly switch places, the tree bending under their weight as they gorge on nectar from the sugar-pink blossom.

A white magnolia with goblet blooms smells of cough mixture. A purple variety glows with colour but offers only a hint of perfume. Another, with white and mauve-striped flowers, is redolent of musky French scent. I count three nests in its branches. If I were a bird, I'd build my nest in this tree, too.

A week later, the magnolia blossoms have mostly dropped, replaced by verdant foliage that camouflages the nests, which may already contain eggs. Blossom is fleeting, but it also symbolises hope and new life.

Spring equinox. The days become longer than the nights as the light returns. My pagan ancestors celebrated equinox as a time of resurrection. Flowers of pink plum, white cherry fall as the fruits swell.

A pair of tūī swoop around the garden, their blue-black wings rustling like taffeta gowns on a Victorian lady as they buzz me. The tūī are exhilarated, and so am I.

It's a beautiful day, so I ride to Ashhurst, where rows of peach and apricot trees flower in the riverside orchard. A field is luminous with bluebells and daffodils.

A convertible Porsche passes me on a roundabout; the roof is down so the middle-aged male driver can enjoy the sunshine. Maybe he's getting a new lease on life. But you don't get more open-top than a bike, and riding through the reawakening countryside is intoxicating. The landscape is experienced best at cycling speed: slow enough to notice, but fast enough to cover ground without the trudgery of walking on concrete.

I stop for a swig of water at Hiwinui School – motto: 'Seeds planted today will flourish and blossom tomorrow.'

On Te Ara Roa walkway, which climbs up behind the university and heads south, bees cluster on hawthorn bushes, elderflowers froth in hedges, and plantains dance in the breeze. The wind scatters birds about the sky. A woman in a yellow tracksuit and a cheery smile resembles a human daffodil. Frogs croak from the pond where swifts fly low, dipping their beaks into the water to drink on the wing, never ceasing their constant movement. I would love to keep on walking, all the way to the end of the land.

Daylight saving begins. An epic band of rain sweeps through the country. Pearlescent sky, white light, silver raindrops. The garden is more and more gorgeous. Blossom in order of appearance: cherry,

plum, apricot, peach, quince, pear, apple. The pear tree, gnarled by
time and bent by the wind, is the most beautiful in the garden when
clothed in curds of creamy blooms.

It's cold this morning, and I don't want to get out of bed. But the day
unfurls, blossoms into sunshine and azure sky, a tūī electric-blue and
black against a yellow kōwhai. Spring continues to manifest itself in
green and gold. New leaves display shades of lime, avocado, pistachio,
pea, asparagus and grass. Flowers gleam the colours of butter,
popcorn, banana skins, and the acid sherbet lemons I loved as a kid.

With daylight saving, the evening feels endless. I go into the
garden and remove grass that has colonised the front border to give
the emerging dusky maroon wallflowers and candy-coloured sweet
peas room to breathe. We always had wallflowers in the garden at
home. Dad loved them, and so do I, because they remind me of
him. I pick snap peas and the thin sprouts of purple broccoli that
my plants have produced in place of the huge uniform heads from
the supermarket. The garden served a function in autumn: to get
me through lockdown. It was a distraction from uncertainty and
isolation, and a source of food. Then, the garden was about survival.
But now it's about pleasure too. I'm happy here. I hear the birds sing,
and inhale the scent of blossom. Who would have thought broad-
bean flowers could smell so sweet?

After being cooped up for so long through winter, I delight in
these small details.

Tiny green fruit on the fig tree. Flush of pale-green growth on the
oak. I walk home across the school field. The children's veggie garden
has been replenished with new plants. The lawnmower man visited
this morning, and the mown-grass scent mingles with the smell of the
onion weed that grows in drifts around the field margins like white

bluebells. Tall, white arum lilies flower on the bank; they're invasive weeds here, far from their native South Africa, but cost $12 a stem if you're buying them for a wedding or funeral in a London florist.

The wind laughs at my bamboo stakes and takes some of the crop. But these sacrificed plants have given me purple-red flowers, delicious perfume, a cover crop to stop other plants taking hold or soil washing away, nectar for insects, and nitrogen that goes back into the ground ready for the greens I'm going to sow next.

In town, an op shop has a yellow, spring-themed window. Others have Christmas displays. I'm momentarily confused. After seventeen years in New Zealand, I still can't adjust to celebrating Christmas in summer. But just as it does in England, the festive consumer frenzy starts at least three months out. Christian festivals replaced old pagan seasonal celebrations; imported to Aotearoa, they sit oddly on the natural cycles. Trying to shoehorn myself into a new calendar has increased my sense of dislocation; the only way to feel at home here is to immerse myself in seasonal rituals that follow the patterns of the year.

How can Kiwi kids understand the meaning of the seasons if the shops are full of Easter bunnies and birds' eggs in autumn, and Halloween pumpkins in spring? Our ancestors were truly dependent on nature. The rites they developed were often a way to worship and appease natural forces in order to survive them.[8] Now the annual cycle of festivals is marked by what's changing in shop windows, not what's happening in the natural world.

I ring Mum and tell her I wish I could come home for Christmas. 'You stay right where you are,' she says.

This morning I make a video call to Karen. I tell her I'm wondering if this virus presents an opportunity to change things dramatically.

People work from home so there's less traffic. We can't travel so there are fewer flights. Shops are closed so we buy less. Less globalisation, more localisation. More appreciation of food. Stronger communities. More gardening.

'Yes,' she says. 'Nature is screaming.'

Then she asks me when I'm coming home. Soon, I say. I'm afraid that less flying means not being able to go to England to see her, or my family. It's hypocritical to expect other people not to travel while doing it myself. I don't know what to do with that fear, or the hypocrisy, so it remains unspoken.

The first rosebud of the year appears on the bushes outside the kitchen. I clear the vegetable beds and, in place of winter cabbage and peas, sow lettuce, rocket and radishes for summer salads. I leave one bed full of self-sown poppies, phacelia, cornflowers, borage and alyssum, for their beauty, and to attract insect pollinators. When they flower, it will be a mass of purple, white and blue.

I pick the first broad beans and eat them raw. They're small, soft, green and subtly flavoured, nothing like the tough, grey-skinned, strongly flavoured beans that traumatised my little sister at the childhood dinner table.

My neighbour mows his lawn. I smell the cut grass and hear the kids playing. The smell and sound take me back to my childhood: cartwheels on the grass, daisies in the lawn, adults talking in deckchairs. In those long summers, I thought things would stay the same forever.

Life swirls in ever-changing patterns, like the kaleidoscope I loved as a kid: always dynamic, sometimes clashing, sometimes flowering into new meaning.

# Bird

... blackbird, happy colonist,
and blacker, sweeter-fluted tui echo
either the other's song.

—MARY URSULA BETHELL, 'The Long Harbour'[1]

**A WAXEYE SWINGS** on the navel orange tree. The orange blossom has a strong bitter-sweet scent, like fancy French soap.

I'm sure I can hear chickens.

My neighbour's been talking about asking the school to remove the tall trees on the field so she can get more light to her solar panels. I know she wants me to write the letter with her. But all morning sparrows have been pulling dried grass from under the apricot tree in the garden, then flying up into the school trees where they're building nests.

The chickens are getting louder.

On the TV news a reporter interviews Sir David Attenborough about his new film, *A Life on Our Planet*.

'It's an obituary for the human race,' says the interviewer.

The broadcast switches back to the studio.

'I can't wait to see that,' says the smiling presenter. Then she's straight into the next item: traffic is gridlocked as school holidays start. Switch to the weather forecast: torrential rain is on its way.

The chickens cluck, and cluck, and cluck.

I go to the university for a real-people-in-a-room workshop. The road around the lagoon is closed for roadworks; the detour takes me through deep mud, and I only just manage to stay on my bike. But I'm glad of the deviation, because as I pass the boathouse a family of greylag geese emerges from the water. I give the geese right of way, then stop to watch two black swans with white-fringed wings, and their four fluffy, dark-grey cygnets. The swans bend their long necks to preen their feathers or filter food from the water. I marvel at their neck construction. Mine feels stiff and sore, and I can hardly look over my right shoulder. Too much sitting at the computer.

A big flock of Canada geese swoops in, skates across the top of the water and lands at the far end. The greylags stand by the water, necks stretched, heads up, honking a warning. As I manoeuvre my bike back on to the road, I pick up a goose feather from the gutter.

A fat kererū wobbles in a crab apple tree across the road from the lagoon, where the kura stood until recently. I used to hear the teenagers singing and smell the toast as I rode past on my way to work. Tall trees have been cut down and the field ploughed up to make way for another development of large houses. Perhaps the kererū has been made homeless. At the university, I spot a woman who lives across the road from me. I ask if those are her chickens I can hear.

'Can you hear them from your place? I'm so sorry! Oh, my poor neighbours!' she says.

I tell her I love the sound of chickens, that I find it soothing and it makes me feel as though I live in the country. When I arrive home that afternoon, there's a box of buff and pale-blue eggs in my mailbox. I leave her a bag of grapefruit and mandarins in return.

I put the goose feather on the windowsill in my study.

I hear a noisy cheeping while walking down my street; in the porch of a house is a yellow budgie in a cage. The imprisoned bird upsets me.

All day I think about the budgie, singing loudly from its prison, unable to fly. I try to understand why anyone would do that to a bird, but I can't find an answer.

When we were sixteen, my friend Caroline and I went to a careers fair. There were so many options, it was a bit overwhelming. But Caroline knew what she wanted to do. We walked up to the aviation stall and she told the man sitting behind the table that she wanted to be a pilot.

The man laughed. 'Women can't be pilots!'

This was the moment I realised that being a woman meant having your wings clipped.

Caroline and I took a trip to the Austrian Alps, just the two of us, before we went off to different universities. It was my first flight, and the first time I'd been away from home without my parents. I took a head-and-shoulders photo of her against a bright blue sky, snowy mountains reflected in her Aviators.

Caroline didn't live long enough to see the monumental shift in society that might have let her follow her dream. She died in a horse-riding accident when we were twenty-five. News of her death made a national newspaper, which described her as a high-flyer.

I'm sitting by the french windows talking to Mum on the phone when I see a ghost train of lights moving slowly across the sky.

'What the hell is that?' I exclaim. I rush to the kitchen windows at the front of the house to follow its progress, then tell Mum I'm going to google it and call her back.

'Make sure you do, so I know you haven't been kidnapped by aliens!' she says.

The lights are Elon Musk's Starlink satellite train. Two thousand active satellites currently orbit the Earth: Musk's project aims to launch between six and twenty-one times more, to beam the internet to every location on the planet.[2] A friend posts on Facebook an animation of all the satellites circling the globe: it's like a busy railway network. Giving everyone access to the internet is an admirable goal, but I can't help thinking that a lot of these satellites will end up as space junk, as our species and our rubbish move further and further outwards into the universe.

The first thing I hear when I wake now is the chickens.

More eggs in the mailbox, and a message: 'We had extra eggs. Found the free rangers' stash under the kowhai tree.'

Simon Barnes' *The Meaning of Birds* devotes a whole chapter to chickens. He describes how fowl have lived alongside humans from the beginnings of civilisation and says there are more chickens on Earth than any other species. Eighteen billion is the estimate he gives.[3] The *New York Times* claims that in 2018 there were about 23 billion chickens on Earth, their combined mass greater than that of all other birds on the planet. The paper reports that scientists reckon our era will be marked by a layer of chicken bones in the fossil record.[4] Chickens, Barnes says, are 'part of the flight from nature, the divorce of humanity from food production, the turning of animals into objects. Chickens are no longer birds, they're McNuggets.'[5]

Scientists are asking whether factory farming caused Covid-19. The *Guardian* reports that industrial farming in China has pushed small-scale farmers to the edge of the forest. As more and more people move into previously undisturbed ecosystems, they contract viruses from animals. The newspaper cites a 2018 study that found most avian flu viruses came from industrialised poultry farming.[6]

Growing up, we kept chickens in a big run at the end of the garden. Sometimes, a fox would slip off the common and get into the henhouse, leaving bloody, feathered carnage. I remember a neighbour coming to kill a chicken so we could eat it for Christmas dinner. Chicken was expensive then, before the days of factory farming. The neighbour wrung the bird's neck and plucked the carcass in the garden, leaving feathers to fly all over the patio.

Poor chickens, always destined to be prey, with no prospect of escape. But better to roam in a world filled with danger than live in a safe but miserable cage.

Heather sends me a link to vote in the Bird of the Year poll. This annual contest was set up to increase awareness of the precarious situation of many New Zealand birds, but it feels futile, picking one, when so many are endangered. Birds designated 'In serious trouble' are:

- Toroa/Antipodean albatross
- Tūturiwhatu/New Zealand dotterel
- Tokoeka/southern brown kiwi
- Tūturiwhatu, kūkuruatu, pohowera/banded dotterel
- Kākāriki karaka/orange-fronted parakeet
- Kaikōura tītī /Hutton's shearwater
- Matuku/bittern
- Kakaruia/black robin
- Kakī/black stilt
- Kākāpō
- Whio/blue duck
- Kiwi pukupuku/little spotted kiwi
- Tara iti/fairy tern
- Hoiho/yellow-eyed penguin
- Mōhua/yellowhead
- Tarāpuka/black-billed gull (the most endangered gull in the world)
- Kōkā/South Island kōkako

The latter was declared extinct in 1967 but a confirmed sighting was made in 2007. The photo on the Bird of the Year website shows a taxidermied museum specimen.

I pick the kakaruia/black robin mainly because it's the most like my favourite English bird, the robin redbreast. We use birds as symbols: the robin is Britain's national bird and regularly tops polls of the country's best beloved.[7] In popular culture they're seen as messengers from loved ones because of their similarity to the first postmen, who wore bright red jackets.

I wake to the dawn chorus.

Riding through the market gardens, an avian cacophony comes from a tall hedge bordering the road. I can hear but not see the birds, except for the odd one or two flying out of the trees above me. The sun is in my eyes and the birds are moving too fast, but I think they're sparrows. Sparrows are always associated with the Cockneys I'm descended from on Mum's side. They are a byword for the commonplace, though they're now endangered in Britain. The roosting sparrows twitter from their tall tree homes that make me think of the tenements in which many Cockneys used to live.

Signs say, 'This is National country. Strong team. More jobs. Better economy.' I guess they mean more roads, more cars and more huge houses. I get that people need somewhere to live, but some developments stipulate a minimum house size. This doesn't help first-time buyers or renters, and it doesn't reduce house prices, which keep increasing. Shouldn't we be down- rather than up-sizing? Progress seems to mean having more of everything. We're constantly exhorted – by governments, councils, corporations, advertising agencies – to keep eating, keep driving, keep buying, keep building, keep consuming. We can't blame the early industrialists and capitalists who started this process: new technologies led to higher standards of living for many people, and could anyone have forseen the negative results? The trouble is, we do know today what industrialisation and consumerism are doing, but we don't seem able to stop.

Back into the outskirts of town, past a takeaway advertising fried chicken: 'Clucking good'. Chicken bones litter the gutter.

When I get home, my neighbour texts to ask if I'd like a sourdough starter. I go round to get it, and as she scrabbles around in the drawer for a plastic container, she says how much she hates all the stuff their household accumulates. We talk about how hard it is to avoid packaging – toys, she says, are especially bad.

Armed with my sourdough starter, I feel as if I'm slowly escaping the grip of consumerism. I'm not alone in this. Since lockdown, more voices are being raised in protest at the destruction of the environment, like birds at dawn, one after another joining the chorus.

Yesterday I pulled grass and Queen Anne's lace out of the front flower border and, thinking of the sparrows taking dead grass for nesting, left some plant strands on the ground. Today I'm pleased to see sparrows take the strands. One male bird keeps loading up his beak with more and more grass, reminding me of Jean-François Millet's 1857 painting *The Gleaners*, in which peasant women scour a field for stray stalks of wheat or corn left from harvest, while a rich man's servants drive away loaded carts in the background. *The Gleaners* was controversial in its day for its commentary on rural poverty, and for highlighting the gap between rich and poor.[8]

I wake at 5.20. A blackbird drops golden notes into the morning. The school is a polling station today, so I walk across the field to vote. Starlings peck around on the grass; they look drab in the shade, but as they fly up, the sun catches their feathers with a flash of metallic-green sheen.

On the way back, something in the grass catches my eye. Not a mushroom, but a bird's egg, pure white. I carry it home cupped in my hand and place it next to the feather on the windowsill.

Later, I ring Mum, and she tells me how as a small child she used to stand in the street looking up at great black clouds of rooks flying to the rookery at Shadyhanger, a piece of woodland that looms over our hometown. Shadyhanger has now been subdivided for a development of five-bedroom homes.

A thrush perches on a branch of the apple tree. I watch his speckled chest rise and fall in time with his song. He's so beautiful, I forget for a moment my annoyance at the rubbish that's blown into the garden. Waxeyes strip open unripe seed pods on the brassicas to get at the green seeds. A bird sings out a single note, pure and clear, over and over.

Birds seem to have taken on a new significance for many people since lockdown. Perhaps it's the quiet, which makes it easier to hear them. Or maybe it's because many of us have more time now. Or could it be that our priorities have changed?

My elder sister tells me she's taken to sitting in the garden in the evenings, listening to the dusk chorus. Her house is next to a normally busy road; she's lived there for more than twenty years and has never heard the birds before.

It's been said that Britain's largest nature reserve is the country's back gardens.[9] I suspect the same claim could be made for Aotearoa. In *Enjoying Nature in the New Zealand Garden* Gordon Ell writes that introduced birds from Europe – blackbirds, sparrows, thrushes, finches – congregate in gardens because they resemble the open woodland of Europe.[10] But it's not just introduced birds that love my garden. Tūī chase sparrows out of the trees in noisy aerial combat; they don't want to share their space with these intruders. A riroriro trills and trills.

A rainy day. I walk on the field in the morning. Shelley is walking too. A broken blue shell and a dead, naked, baby bird lie on the path. The bird is so small, so vulnerable; I can't bear that anyone might squash it, or throw it, so I gently move it onto the grass with my foot.

'Baby bird. Black one,' says Shelley, pointing to the tree.

Heather and I drive to Foxton to see the kuaka/godwits in the Manawatū River estuary, which is listed under the Ramsar Convention on Wetlands as a Wetland of International Importance. The estuary is salt marsh and mudflat, and is an important feeding ground for many birds, including the bar-tailed godwit, which every year flies non-stop from its breeding grounds in Alaska to Aotearoa to escape the harsh northern winter.[11] This year, one of the birds has broken the world record for the longest avian migration, flying 12,200 kilometres in eleven days, its journey lengthened by strong easterly winds.[12]

We park on the street, then walk to a viewing platform that looks out over the mudflats. Two women and a man are looking at the birds through telescopes. My little opera glasses seem inadequate, so I put them back in my coat pocket, feeling embarrassed. One of the women has a particularly powerful telescope. Heather comments on it, and the woman, who has a Lancashire accent, lets us look through it. The kuaka are mostly standing on one leg with their heads tucked under their wings. The woman says she's been coming here for years but the number of birds isn't what it used to be: the most godwits she's seen at one time is 250, a few years ago. It's impossible to count the birds but I'd say there are way fewer than a hundred today.

The birds come here to feed over the summer, fattening up for their long journey home.

'They were little dumplings when they left,' the woman says.

She points out wrybills further out; they're small grey-and-white birds with black collars and distinctive sideways-curved bills (the only bird in the world with this feature). The woman says there are spoonbills too, self-introduced from Australia, far off on the spit in the middle.

I look in vain for a few minutes, then the woman lines up the telescope for me, and I see the large, long-legged white bird with its head turned towards me, showing the outline of its extraordinary spoon-shaped black beak, which it uses to catch fish and crabs.

After a while, Heather and I walk along the pathway that skirts the wetland. An interpretation board tells us that the wetland is home to many types of fish, including threatened species, and forms a migratory path to the sea for all native fish in the Manawatū River catchment. Archaeologists have also found remains here of the semi-nomadic moa-hunter culture, dating from 1400–1650 AD.

A sign says of this place: 'Modern people find it a soulful place to visit'. The soulful effect is diminished for us by off-road vehicles driving on the beach.

We stop at the café on the way home. Heather says hello to someone as we walk in, then says to me with a nod of her head, 'It's the bird lady'. The woman from Lancashire is having lunch with a man in the corner. Heather and I drink tea and eat bread and butter pudding to fortify ourselves for the trip back to Palmy. Suddenly, a swift flies into the room and flits from window to window. The bird lady gets up and ushers the swift towards the door and then it's gone, like a dark arrowhead.

I read that the great Māori navigator Kupe followed the migratory route of the kuaka to reach Aotearoa. When the birds were seen leaving Piwhane (now Spirits Bay), the northernmost point of Aotearoa, for their return journey, they were seen to symbolise the spirits of the Māori dead returning to their homeland of Hawaiki.[13]

I'm on to another bird book: Matt Merritt's *A Sky Full of Birds*. Merritt notes that migratory birds live in perpetual motion, bound to the seasons and to their invisible global routes, regardless of weather. This endless movement, he says, is both curse and blessing for the birds, but fascinates us, who are bound 'by the ties of family, work, place and culture'.[14]

England is going into full lockdown again as Covid cases rise. From my bedroom window I see an Air New Zealand plane in magpie livery flying towards the airport. We're rediscovering our freedom while much of the world is still captive, hiding away from a lethal virus. Like the migratory birds, my urge to fly has been both blessing – that I'm safely in Aotearoa – and curse – that if I leave, I can't return. And like these avian migrants, I'm also bound by unseen ties to two countries.

To Linton at lunchtime, where a new sign at the army camp says 'Defence Force Property. Entry on business only'. Birds soar above, unconstrained by signs and boundaries. I turn around and almost ride into the ditch while watching geese pass overhead in V formation. The birds fly across the stream, up, up and over the pine trees on the crest of the hill, until they're lost to sight, heading beyond the Manawatū River as it flows endlessly west, past the city spread out below with its roads and cars and buildings and clocktower, over my garden, then beyond the Manawatū plains, the fields and the creeping housing developments, buoyed by the wind, through the clouds, onwards into the sun until they are gone. Where are they going, these geese? I think of the birds flying away to their northern homes, taking part in the great ebb and flow of life across the globe. They make me feel restless. I used to be part of this continuous movement, but now I must stay put. I want to fly away too, though I know I have freedom that friends in England envy. And this strange year has freed me in another way: from a corporate life of eight hours a day trapped in an office, from near-total dependence on an agrichemical food supply. There's no complete escape from work and supermarket in our world, but this feels like the start of a new way of living.

Labour Day. It's hot so I put winter things away: gloves, hats, heater, door sausages, slippers.

A red-and-black poppy blooms in the garden. I spear the garden fork into the new vegetable bed and turn over the compost. It's brimful of creatures carrying out their daily tasks of recycling and rebuilding our planet. Fat red worms wriggle away from the light in alarm. Ants carry eggs to safety. Tiny grey spiders scurry. I plant out the tomatoes: 'Black Krim', 'Brandywine', 'Green Zebra', 'Yellow Pear'. The compost feels warm as I dig holes and plant the seedlings, firming them down, like tucking a small child under a duvet.

I was too hasty putting away the winter things. Today is cold and wet. I feel cooped up, and in the evening I walk on the field. The path is covered in worms that have been flushed out of their burrows by the rain. A big flock of gulls passes silently overhead. I love the pattering of rain on the hood of my raincoat. And I love equally the feeling of coming back into the warm house, getting into pyjamas, and sitting wrapped in a blanket in the chair by the window with a book and a cup of tea. I know this is exactly what Mum is doing, too, on the other side of the world.

A splash of red in the grass: the wind has blown the petals off the poppy. The lives of flowers are ephemeral, as short as those of World War I soldiers who left their uneventful lives for the adventure of a lifetime. My grandfathers were lucky to survive.

I cycle into the countryside. A fence has a bird box on top of every post; a starling sits on each box, calling its *clack clack clack*. A mother duck waddles across the road, followed by four ducklings. I brake, but there's a car coming the other way. This is a fast road, and I think about indicating to the driver to slow down, but he sees me, sees the ducklings, and stops. We smile at each other, and he waves. The ducklings reach safety on the other side of the road.

Shortly afterwards, something smacks into the back of my head. What the hell? A territorial magpie has divebombed me. The bird flies up, turns around and comes back for a second go, skimming the top of my helmet. The close call is a thrill, and I laugh in surprise and relief as the bird takes off, but I pedal like mad, out of its territory, away from its nest, crouched low to avoid another skirmish.

Back through Kelvin Grove, where carved pumpkins sit on gates and ghosts decorate windows. Celebrating Halloween in spring messes with my orientation again. The origins of Halloween lie in the ancient Celtic festival of Samhain, marking the end of summer. The boundary between the worlds of the living and the dead was thought to become thin on this night, when the ghosts of the departed returned to Earth. I like Halloween, but can't be enthusiastic about it when sky-blue birds' eggs are falling from trees and blossom bedecks the hedgerows.

In the Celtic spring festival of Beltane, unlike Halloween, light triumphs over darkness. Beltane is marked by the arrival of the migratory cuckoo; in Aotearoa this is mirrored in the return of the pīpīwharauroa/shining cuckoo.[15] Druid priests burnt sacrificial crops and animals on huge bonfires as offerings to the gods and made predictions about the future. The bonfires drove out lingering pestilence and welcomed the cleansing power of the sun. Beltane was also the time to venture out into the world after winter hibernation, visiting people and making merry at spring fairs.[16]

I'm not going to sacrifice anything on a bonfire, but in the spring sunshine I feel myself emerging from winter like a bird unfolding its wings.

# Wind

This is the weather for travelling south,
Into the fresh blue sky,
With clouds like gossamer flying,
Paddocks rounded as an eiderdown,
Wind flowing over the tawny grass,
Swinging, swinging,
Boisterous as children
In the boughs of the dark wind-breaks.
—RUTH DALLAS, 'On the Road'[1]

**THE GALES THAT ACCOMPANY** spring in Manawatū are howling. We sit just inside the Roaring Forties, a belt of wind circling westwards around the bottom of the globe at latitude 40. Manawatū has been formed by wind, carved into shape by the predominant westerly, which bends trees and hedges to the east as if they're praying. There is no forgetting the wind here. It swoops into the region, shakes things up, then continues on its way. The wind bowls heavy objects down the street, whistles around buildings, makes it hard to stand upright. When walking, you must hunker low to the ground to avoid being lifted off your feet, *Wizard of Oz* style. But I miss it in winter, when heavy smog hangs over the city from woodburners turned up against the damp cold. And in summer I wish it would return to freshen the hot, dense air.

A broken window latch in my bedroom bangs against the frame. As I try to fix it, I see the fruit trees whipping around, immature fruit dropping to the grass. The wind takes a tithe – it did, after all, blow some of the soil here. The fertile plains of Manawatū were formed by the westerly picking up silt and depositing it across the region.[2]

I don't really own this patch of land any more than our community stakeholders own the river. We just get to live on the soil, and by the river, for a little while.

Today is the first of November: el Día de Muertos, or the Day of the Dead. A large monarch butterfly sails past the window. I read that monarchs are indigenous to the Americas but are classified as natives in New Zealand because they arrived without human intervention. Scientists think monarchs were carried by cyclones west from America, across the Pacific, via smaller islands to Australia, and from there to Aotearoa.[3] In America, monarchs make one of the longest annual migrations of any insect: up to 5000 kilometres from Canada to Mexico. En route, the butterflies feed on the nectar of specific flowers that bloom at the time of their migration – a beautiful example of interdependence of species. But monarch numbers are dwindling. Their favoured food sources are declining because of herbicides; their migration routes are being disrupted by extreme weather events caused by climate change; and in Mexico the forests in which monarchs overwinter are being cut down. Monarchs have a special significance to Mexicans: millions of the butterflies arrive on el Día de Muertos, and are said to be the returning souls of departed loved ones.[4]

A dozen or so people stand in the Memorial Park car park on a Tuesday lunchtime. We're here for a local history tour. Most are older people, for whom this local history is within living memory.

The park is being overhauled, but our guide, Jason, a council parks planner, tells us the work is on hold: 'The lottery money didn't come through because of Covid-19.' He says that when work starts up again, a war memorial theme will be built into the new playground, with poppies in the flooring design and play equipment; a gun donated by the army; and a heroes' walk remembering those who kept the home fires burning. The council wants to recreate a 1950s feel: 'We want to make it fun, optimistic, lively and colourful. The development going forward is based on the past.'[5]

Jason tells us that tree roots have caused undulations that affect the play equipment. Over the past ten years, dozens of trees have been torn down, the land bulldozed and flattened. Shade sails will take the trees' place.

'Shame,' says the group.

Most of the attendees have stories about the park. One woman remembers kids chalking the pavement to play hopscotch. Another has brought an iPad on which she shows us photos of herself as a girl in the 1960s, doing double splits in the air – on roller skates.

'I was once offered sweets by a man to walk with him down to the duck pond,' she says.

Her comment prompts Jason to talk about the trees again. 'The problem with the trees was the sightlines. To make people feel safe we took the trees out.'

We walk past the pond, where the odd, low roaring of mating Australian bell frogs comes from an island of plants in the middle. This makes me think about how the Duck Pond sign at the entrance regularly has the D scratched out and replaced with an F. And I think about the man who propositioned me there during lockdown.

I go to campus with workmates for a tree planting to commemorate our late colleague. We've chosen a maple, with red, star-shaped leaves, to reflect her Canadian heritage. We all place soil in the planting hole. We're offered a spade, but I move the mulch and dirt with my bare hands: I want to feel the earth, get it under my nails, connect with the soil and the tree and my lost friend.

A workmate quotes from 'To a Child Dancing in the Wind' by W.B. Yeats:

*Dance there upon the shore;*
*What need have you to care*
*For wind or water's roar?*[6]

On the way home, as I approach He Ara Kotahi bridge, a little girl on roller skates spins in the wind like a top, throwing her arms out, her yellow skirt flying up around her legs.

*Te Ara* tells of the origins of the weather.[7] Tāwhirimātea, the Māori god of wind and storms, was the son of Papatūānuku (earth mother) and Ranginui (sky father). Tāwhirimātea's brothers forced their parents to separate, so that light would enter the world. Tāwhirimātea was so angry about this split that he produced numerous children – the spirits of winds, storms and rain – to wage war on his brothers. Tāwhirimātea sent his wind children to the four corners of the Earth: Tūāraki to the north, Tonga to the south, Marangai to the east and Hauāuru to the west. The spirits snapped trees, whipped up waves and wrecked crops. But Tāwhirimātea's brother Tūmatauenga, the god of war and humans, cast spells to help people fight the wind. To this day, his charges, the people of Aotearoa, continue to battle the weather.

The day is muggy; the temperature gets up to 24 degrees. It's US election day; the results are tantalisingly close, and I call on Heather for moral support. We arrange to meet at a café, and I walk into town.

An elderly woman leans on a wall, shopping trolley at her side.

'Are you all right there?' I ask her.

'Just waiting for the wind to stop,' she says.

Some hope, I think. I press on while the woman waits, gathering her breath for another push.

At the café, Heather tells me there are rumours that the Canada geese at the lagoon are going to be culled because they shit on the ground. I tell her there's human shit in the lagoon, and she says, yes, there's a sign on the bridge.

Canada geese were introduced to New Zealand as a gift from US President Theodore Roosevelt early in the twentieth century.[8] At one time they were thought to be extinct in North America because of over-hunting. Conservation efforts brought the geese back from the brink, and introduced them to new areas, where they continue to clash with humans over territory and resources.[9]

Tired of trying to understand the US election – the mechanics of electoral colleges and swing states, and how so many millions of people could vote for a man like Donald Trump – I go for a twilight ride. I head west into the sunset, along the river path to He Ara Kotahi; the sky is layered orange, blue and black. It's busy at the bridge: people are drawn towards its lights like moths. Three girls take selfies. A young couple wrapped around each other face out towards the water. A man leans on a bike decorated with a string of blue lights; a boom box on his carrier rack plays 'The Ballad of John and Yoko', banned in some parts of the US for its reference to crucifixion. The man tips his head back and exhales a long stream of vapour.

I ride back to the crackle and fizz of fireworks.

Guy Fawkes' Day. The little boy across the street tells me, 'We're having fireworks tonight! 'Cos there was this man, and he went to prison 'cos he tried to bomb the Beehive.'

In England we knew Guy Fawkes' Day as Bonfire Night. It's another of those events thought to have been superimposed on a pagan festival – in this case Samhain, with its cleansing bonfires to ward off evil.[10] Perhaps it was politically expedient to combine this old ritual with a new one that celebrated the defeat of an attempt to oust the government in a time of religious and political division.

The rain starts at five and continues all evening. The council fireworks display is postponed, but people let off fireworks on the field and in their gardens.

The paths through the woods behind the university are muddy; I slip and slide along. Two teenage girls wearing headphones jog towards me. I say hello to the first girl, but I don't think she hears me, and the second doesn't look in my direction.

A woman and a little blonde girl in a pink dress sprigged with white flowers come up the steps towards me. The girl carries a blue seaside bucket; she picks up a leaf.

'What are you collecting in your bucket?' I ask, but she's shy and doesn't answer.

'Treasures!' says her mother.

'There are lots of treasures in these woods,' I reply.

'There are lots at home too,' the mum says wryly.

I also collect some treasures on my walk: a black feather, a smooth pebble, a pinecone. Like a magpie, I pick up things that catch my eye. I take them home and add them to my collection on the windowsill.

The US election is finally over. Delivering her victory speech, Kamala Harris, the first female vice-president of the US, wears a white trouser suit in tribute to the suffragettes who fought for women's right to vote.

Harris says, 'Every little girl watching tonight sees that this is a country of possibilities.'[11]

The garden brims with orange marigolds, red poppies, blue cornflowers, double and single purple poppies, and shiny yellow buttercups among the prickly gooseberries with their green fruit – Dad's favourite, and mine. The lawn is a field of daisies.

A couple of tūī bomb around the garden and field, perfectly in sync with each other's movements. The roses are in full bloom. A

'Crepuscule' covers the trellis with large, sunset-coloured blooms; three pearl-white 'Iceberg' bushes in the border fling petals across the driveway; the blushing 'Wedding Bells' climber frames the french windows; a tiny rambler with the palest pink blooms pulses perfume, although its vicious thorn, embedded in my finger, once required two sets of antibiotics.

Strolling through the city in November, it's easy to see why Palmerston North was once known as Rose City. The slogan related to the rose trial grounds in the esplanade, a fragrant heaven of apricot, burgundy, coral, lavender and gold in summer. But roses grow all around the neighbourhood too: a tiny variety poking through a fence, its blooms so far along the yellow spectrum they're almost green; voluptuous, peach-coloured beauties sprawling in a border; long-stemmed, elegant acid-yellow roses clipped into formal standards in a front lawn; hot-pink blooms scrambling boldly through a tree; and the deepest blood-red, velvety, romantic rose climbing up a shed. The city is en fête. Today's light breeze carries the scent of the roses towards me: liquorice, clove, lemon, violet. I inhale it, because soon the bushes will be whirling in a gale and the flowers will be gone.

I've always loved roses, so long used as an emblem in England: at school I learnt about the white rose of York and the red rose of Lancaster, and how they were combined into the Tudor rose to symbolise the unity of two warring clans.

Armistice Day. I join the small crowd gathered at the Cenotaph at 10.45. At eleven, a hush descends and the clocktower bells chime.

Speakers draw parallels between today's pandemic and the Spanish flu of 1918. We're told that celebrations marking the end of the Great War were banned in Auckland to stop the virus spreading.

Colonel Stefan Michie from Linton Camp says, 'United as a community we can all emerge to a brighter future.'

A cold front moves in. I wake up extra early with freezing feet.

Children play soccer on the field; a couple of girls huddle into their hoodies by the goalposts. The roar of the wind lifts the children's screams high into the air.

I struggle against the wind on my lunchtime walk round the neighbourhood. A wind chime tinkles. It's recycling day, and escaped rubbish flies around the street. It's not just litter that bowls along in the gale – the recycling bins have mostly been blown over too. A gust of wind almost lifts me off my feet. At the traffic lights, I hold on to the streetlamp while waiting to cross.

The city's roses shiver in the wind. My white 'Icebergs' turn brown and bedraggled in the wet. Rain, hail and gales grow stronger over the evening.

I umm and ahhh about the weather but am desperate to get out for a ride. There's a strong westerly, so I head east. Deserted river path. *Cyclists this is not a race track.* There's no one about. I speed up. Wheeee! Through the market gardens. Warm, salty aroma of cows, and spicy smell of celery from the fields. A burnt-out car and fresh black tyre marks on the road. Smoke from a bonfire hazes the road ahead. A bird of prey swoops, white in the light. Wind whistles across the fields; it's so strong it blows my helmet back from my forehead. Gusts push me out into the road. I tack into the wind like a yacht. Traffic is sparse but every time a car approaches I'm worried I'm going to be barrelled into its path. I abandon the road and head back to the river. Safely home, I check my Strava cycling app. Personal Best out, Personal Worst back.

Since I started cycling (after my car died), wind is no longer just wind. It's a strong westerly, an occasional easterly, or a chilly southerly straight from the Antarctic; a head wind, tail wind or side wind. My ear-warmer is in the wash, so today I'm bare-eared. The geese sit by the lagoon with their heads tucked under their wings, the draught ruffling their feathers. A pile of goslings sleeps on the grass.

Along the river path, bare willow branches clatter. The roiling river is the colour of milky tea. I tug down the zip of my rain jacket just as I reach the bridge, where the wind thunders off the river; it turns the coat-flaps into a sail. My ears start to hurt. I stop to get my breath back under the pine trees at the top of the hill. The wind soughs through the branches. Swifts are tossed around the sky.

A mountain biker bombs past. 'Too windy for this, eh?' he shouts.

But it's not; it's exhilarating. I get back on my bike, and the wind pushes me up the hill, a hand in my back.

The wind can be friend as well as foe.

The westerlies that blast across Manawatū are funnelled through and amplified by the Manawatū Gorge. In *Ravaged Beauty*, Catherine Knight explains how the technology to harness this free power source arrived in the region in 1999 with New Zealand's first wind farm, just south of the gorge. And just as the gorge divides the mountain range, the growth of the region's wind farms split the community. In 2003, a larger wind farm was built to the north of the gorge. In 2004, another proposed farm triggered a battle between residents concerned about noise and visual pollution and the farm owners, Aotearoa New Zealand Wind Farms. The Environment Court found in favour of the wind farms. The Turitea Wind Farm proposal in 2008 was different. While earlier farms had been sited in the Tararua Range – a modified agricultural landscape of 'low' or 'medium' significance – part of the Turitea farm was destined for indigenous bushland. This time, a government board of inquiry gave consent for only sixty of the proposed 131 turbines. Work started in 2019. At the same time, another proposal was abandoned after the

Environment Court gave consent for only seventy of 127 proposed turbines.

Significantly, this wasn't an 'environment versus economy' debate, but one that pitted environmentalists against environmentalists, those in favour of renewable energy against those who wanted to conserve the landscape.[12]

I like the region's iconic windmills spinning on the ranges, and we need renewable energy to meet climate goals. But there must be a better way to do this than by sacrificing ancient landscapes to economic growth. Perhaps, first, we should reduce our energy usage. And there's a sense of intrusion and imposition in this story that makes me uncomfortable: powerful corporations bringing change to a small community, an external force pushing in, like the wind itself.

Today is hot, cold, wet and dry in turns, but always windy. On campus, a broken blue umbrella has been stuffed in a bin. A broken red umbrella sticks out of the next bin.

At the Sustainability Club community garden the plot overflows with self-seeded spinach and yellow and red chard, despite the groundskeepers' best efforts with the weedkiller. I harvest vegetables, hearing only wind and birdsong. A duck and eleven ducklings waddle past. A thrush sifts through dead leaves. Pīwakawaka, rainbow parakeets, tūī and blackbirds pass overhead.

I pick a spray of 'Wedding Bells' roses from the garden, and put them in a vase by Mum and Dad's wedding photo taken in spring 1959. My parents were just shy of their twenty-fifth wedding anniversary when Dad's heart stopped forever. He was fifty-six, a year older than I am now.

On the back deck, 'Chameleon' roses turn from bright lemon to pale yellow to vermilion to flushed pink to speckled white before the petals fall and scatter on the breeze. But this is not the end: in the petals' place, tiny rosehips grow, full of seeds. The wind blows away the old and brings in the new.

I look out across the field. A pink, blue and grey sunset; dark clouds scudding across the sky. A little girl runs out on to the soccer pitch and turns cartwheels on the grass, arms and legs spinning like a turbine in the wind.

# Summer

Tree—Weed—Insect

# Tree

You can see that trees
know how it is
to be bound
into the earth
and how it is to rise defiantly
into the sky.

—DINAH HAWKEN, 'Hope'[1]

**THE PLUM TREE DOMINATES** the view from my kitchen, filling the window frame with a dark green vista.

I spend a lot of time sitting by the window, eating, reading, drinking tea, talking to friends. And watching: I've observed the tree's comings and goings all year. It's a complete ecosystem, providing home and sustenance to insects, birds and humans. Often, when I'm coming down my street, I hear a thrush singing from the topmost branches, and I know I'm nearly home.

Another plum tree grows at the back of the garden; when I'm working at the computer in the back room, I hear an occasional thunk as maroon-green plums drop onto the garage roof. This tree is covered in fruit year in year out. I use a long-handled pruning cutter to reach some of the plums at the top of the tree. Even after I've filled four baskets, the birds will get more than me.

There's a nest in this tree that's made of coconut fibres from my hanging baskets, interwoven with strands of green plastic. The bird has taken an assortment of bits and pieces from here and there and made them into a home.

For my birthday, an English friend who lives in Palmerston North gives me two rocks; she's painted one with a pīwakawaka ('I believe I can fly') and one with a tree ('Love where you live').

'One is for when you want to go home, and one is for when you want to stay,' she says. I put them in my nature collection.

I take the day off and sit in the garden reading. In *The Meaning of Trees*, Robert Vennell tells how Polynesian migrants arrived in Aotearoa about 750 years ago, when it was a land of forest brimming with harakeke, pōhutukawa, karaka, huge tree ferns and towering kauri.[2]

But Aotearoa's forests were in trouble from the minute humans arrived. Polynesian settlers burnt off trees to clear land for crop cultivation, and by 1840, 40 percent of the native tree cover was gone. The carnage intensified with the arrival of Europeans, who took out a quarter of the remaining forest between 1890 and 1900.[3]

Many European colonists arriving in Manawatū to take up their allocated blocks of land found not a grassy, pastoral scene but dense bush. In some places it was so thick that settlers couldn't find their blocks. While some gave up, opting for town life instead, others cleared the land by burning down the trees.[4] I can't criticise these people; they removed trees to grow crops so they could survive. They overcame hardships I can't imagine to create the society I live in, and benefit from.

New Zealanders began to see the value of indigenous forest as a tourist attraction at the beginning of the twentieth century. But, sadly for Manawatū, the region wasn't scenic enough to attract tourists, and most of its green cloak of forest was lost. Between 1878 and 1908, pasture increased from 5 percent of Manawatū land cover to more than 50 percent.[5]

Not everyone had the mantra of economic progress at the cost of the trees. Vennell says that for both Māori and new generations of Pākehā, trees became 'powerful symbols of what it means to live in New Zealand, from the lonely, stoic cabbage tree on the farm to the primeval kauri forests of Northland and the dripping-wet beech forests of Fiordland'.[6]

We use trees to orientate ourselves to our homelands, just as we use birds. In Aotearoa, tōtara is symbolic of a mighty chieftain, and is used in the eulogy:

*Kua hinga te tōtara i Te Waonui a Tāne.*
*A tōtara has fallen in the great forest of Tāne.*[7]

Māori prized tōtara for building waka, because of its durability, strength and ease of carving. One tree could make a war canoe big enough to carry a hundred warriors into battle.[8]

Oak is king of the British woodland in the same way that tōtara is chief of the forest in Aotearoa. Oak signifies fortitude and endurance. And just as tōtara was carved into waka, oak was used to build the ships in which the British Navy went to war. Celts worshipped the oak tree, and acorns are still considered good-luck charms. Some European colonists who came to New Zealand carried their heritage and memories encased inside acorns in their baggage. Perhaps they were carrying them for luck, too, on the dangerous sea voyage.

In 1883, John Batchelar planted an English acorn on his Palmerston North estate. He's alleged to have said, 'By the time this oak is grown, it will be wood for my coffin'.[9] But when Batchelar died, the tree was spared, and it still stands on a patch of grass next to the science park.

I pay the tree a visit. A woman sits on one of two wooden benches beneath its branches. It feels somehow disrespectful to lean my bike against the trunk, so I prop it against the empty bench. Others appear not to have the same reverence: a beer bottle and folded paper takeaway bag are tucked behind the plaque at the base of the tree that commemorates its planting. The oak is enormous; I try to take a photo but can't fit the whole tree into my viewfinder. I want to hug the oak, but it's a workday, and there are people in the surrounding offices, and students coming in and out of the flats. I make do with just touching its bark. A few smaller – but still big – oaks grow around this tree; its offspring probably. Epiphytes scramble up their trunks. I pick up three acorns, for good luck; they'll join my windowsill nature collection.

A tree is solid, living history, composed of layers, holding on to the whakapapa of a place. Maybe this is why we say 'family tree'. In its 138-year lifetime, Batchelar's oak has seen five generations of humans come and go, all with their dreams and aspirations, hopes and fears.

Near Batchelar's oak tree, behind the university dairy farm and horticultural science labs and greenhouses on Batchelar Road, stands a karaka grove. I park my bike against the chain-metal fence that surrounds the university buildings, then I read the interpretation board that gives a history of the site. It says that the land south of the Manawatū River was once native forest, which was partly cleared by Māori settlers. Rangitāne cultivated large karaka orchards here in pre-European days. According to tradition, Māori brought karaka with them from Hawaiki. Karaka was a valuable food, but despite its tempting sweet smell, the kernel is toxic, and the yellow and orange fruit is inedible without a lengthy preparation process involving multiple soakings and boiling.[10]

The board says that in 1860 Rangitāne sold land here to Batchelar. Rangitāne chief Hoani Meihana Te Rangiotū told Batchelar that in 1820, when he was a baby, this place had been the scene of a great battle between his and another tribe. Te Rangiotū only narrowly escaped death. Batchelar promised to retain six karaka trees as a Rangitāne memorial.

In 1981, the university's Horticultural Science department built a garden beneath the trees, and the grove later opened to the public.

Three carved pou named Te Koha o te Whenua (the Gift of the Land) were designed in the form of a pātaka kai to ensure rich harvests. The grove commemorates the past while symbolising future life.[11]

I walk through a steel entranceway, shaped like a pātaka, into the grove. Outside noise is filtered out; it's cool, dark and peaceful here. Native ferns grow in the shade, and new karaka seedlings pop up from the soil. I sit on a bench commemorating Eileen Earle of the horticulture department, and her passion for native plants. A lone bird calls. I feel a sense of – there's no other word for it – spirituality.

After a while, I ride back to He Ara Kotahi bridge, which was designed to resemble a karaka to celebrate the tree's importance to the area.[12] The design also refers to the Rangitāne ancestor Hau, who threw a tree across the river to use as a bridge as he chased his errant wife.[13] The roots of the bridge-tree are on the south bank of the river, while its canopy rests on the north side. To me, the bridge resembles an axis mundi, a world tree, linking heaven and earth.

I ride north across the bridge; up through the karaka branches towards my personal paradise. The pine forest at the top of the Linton bike track is my favourite part of the ride. The traffic noise doesn't reach this far: the deep green silence is broken only by the wind soughing through the treetops. I sit down, leaning against a tree trunk, listening to the wind passing through the millions of needle-like leaves. Kawakawa and elder saplings grow through the carpet of pine needles on the forest floor.

Two people are picking things up from the ground and loading them into a bike trailer.

'Are you collecting pinecones?' I ask one of them.

'Yes, it's great foraging here! We get loads of cones. I love it up here.'

'Yeah, me too, I like to sit here and listen to the wind.'

'Yes, it's therapeutic, isn't it?' she replies, before they ride off with their fuel.

The ground is soft, the sun shines on my legs, and I shut my eyes. The woods are unknown, mysterious and alluring. The light slants down through the tall tree trunks, and I feel as if I'm in a fairytale forest. But what happens if, as in a fairy tale, I lose my way home? Many European fairy stories play out against forests that harbour wolves, witches, bears, dragons and dark secrets. I remember what Jason said on the Memorial Park tour: 'To make people feel safe, we took the trees out.' The originals of many of these stories end in violence and death, although the versions lots of us knew in childhood were sanitised with a happy ending: the lost children saved by a virtuous forester; the persecuted young woman rescued by a handsome prince.

Perhaps those of us who come from Europe but now live elsewhere orientate ourselves to pine woods and oak trees as a way of clinging on to remembered places that no longer exist, except in our imaginations.

Summer solstice, the high point to which the year has been building. The word solstice comes from Latin, meaning 'the sun stands still'; it refers to the way the sun seems to hang in the sky for a brief pause in its journey around the planet before reversing direction. To pagans this marked the moment when the world began its descent back into darkness, and it was a sign that they needed to prepare food for winter.

The red plums are ready. My neighbour and I swelter in our kitchens, making sauce, jam and chutney to keep us through the rest of the year.

Tonight sees the culmination of the Great Conjunction, when the solar system's two giant planets, Saturn and Jupiter, pass so close to each other that they look as one from Earth. This will be the closest the planets have passed in four hundred years, and the first time the conjunction has been visible to almost the whole world in eight centuries. The Star of Bethlehem, believed by Christians to have foretold the birth of Christ and the first Christmas, is thought to have been the Conjunction.[14]

It's a disappointingly cloudy night for stargazing, but just as I look out of the window a sliver of moon appears between clouds and one star shines more brightly than the others. I don't know if I'm seeing the Conjunction or another star, but I tell myself I've witnessed a once-in-eight-hundred-years event. I think of the generations of people who've seen this same occurrence, all of us bound together in a web of humanity, citizens of an immense universe. The last time the planets were seen to pass so closely was in 1226.[15] This was about the time the first Polynesian migrants discovered Aotearoa. Did they consider this star a portent too?

But while the planets appear close, they're still hundreds of millions of kilometres apart.

Pōhutukawa – New Zealand Christmas trees – flare red along the city streets on a blue-sky morning. I go to campus carrying tinsel for our friend's commemorative maple tree, but someone has already decorated its branches for Christmas. The tree sparkles in place of her.

The arboretum is cool and green, like the inside of an emerald. The first cicadas start to call. Fluffy white cottonwood seeds float through the air, settling on bushy firs like snow on a Christmas tree. It's snowing for real in England. I sit by the river and talk to Mum on the phone. Today is her eighty-first birthday. In the northern hemisphere it's winter solstice.

'Trust me to be born on the shortest day of the year,' she says.

I remind her that her birthday marks the start of light returning to the world.

After hanging up, I walk along the dusty gravel pathway that runs through the university farms out to the state highway. I pick fragrant honeysuckle that twines through the hedges; its perfume reminds me of the bath cubes and talc we used to buy Mum at Christmas when we were kids. This is the time of year I miss my family most. I worry about whether I'll be able to get back to England to spend time with Mum, before it's too late. When I ring now, I always ask her questions about the past, but sometimes she says she can't remember much of it. If you lose your memories, does the past disappear too?

On Sundays when I was a child, Dad used to take us on family walks through Pitch Place, a gloomy section of the common filled with towering pines. Dad grew up here, and he knew these woods like the back of his hand. We gathered pinecones, mostly to use as kindling for the fire, but the best cones we painted and covered with glitter to hang on the tree at Christmas. The cones, and other treasured Christmas decorations, were stored in Dad's old iron RAF trunk.

Dad taught Mum to drive in Pitch Place in a square, lumpy-looking white Austin Maxi hatchback with all four of us in the back. Mum used Vaseline hand cream, and always carried a pink plastic bottle of it in her handbag. Its perfume was cloying in the close confines of the car. Dad smoked roll-ups, and even though he opened his window to let the sickly-sweet smoke out, the inside of the car was a fug of cigarettes and artificial fragrance. No wonder I got carsick. The memory of it still makes me nauseous. If it was a particularly bumpy ride, we'd beg Mum to stop, then pile out and run off in the opposite direction, sheltering behind the trees and screaming with laughter and fright as the Maxi bunny-hopped across the forest floor.

In the woods, the smell of pines was intense. People say pine smells fresh and antiseptic, like cleaning fluid, but to me it was a festering, earthy scent of fallen branches, damp black leaves and decaying pine needles that signified a dark and slightly mysterious place, haunted by the ghosts of previous generations.

That smell was the backdrop to Dad's life. He spent his childhood roaming those pine woods with his three brothers. During World War II, the common was used as an army training ground by troops preparing for the D-Day invasion, and the tank tracks cut through the ferny undergrowth are still there. When the fighting was over, Dad worked as a forester with the two brothers who'd survived it.

Then Dad met Mum, and when children came along we all moved to the house with the huge garden backing on to the common. When Dad wasn't at work he was building things from wood: a playhouse for my sisters and me; a shed for my brother; a hutch for the rabbits; and a large coop for the chickens. He cut logs for the fire, and selected the perfect pine tree at Christmas, ready for us to hang with glittered pinecones.

Despite the urban, semi-detached council house and small garden that became our home for the last eight years of his life, Dad never really left the woods behind. He still took us – as initially reluctant teenagers – to the common for Sunday walks. He still chopped logs for the fire. And every year he still brought home a real Christmas tree that we hung with glittered pinecones. Dad's been gone nearly forty years now, but whenever I catch that scent, I still think of him.

I haven't bothered with a Christmas tree since I moved to New Zealand. It doesn't feel right, in the middle of summer. I put up a tree-shaped advent calendar instead, then stand all the cards I receive along the mantelpiece. One card (from Heather) features a kererū in a pōhutukawa; another (from Mum) a robin redbreast in a holly tree. I decorate the house with berryless summer holly branches from the garden. While I'm cutting the holly, I see Shelley on the field. I wave and signal her to wait, then cut some hydrangeas and take them to her.

'Happy Christmas!'

'Thank you! Happy Christmas!'

Not celebrating Christmas in the traditional way is liberating. Instead of joining the crush at the shops, I cycle around to see friends, delivering jam and chutney and bags of plums. In return I receive a jar of homemade sauerkraut (labelled 'White Butterfly: contains cabbage, salt, juniper berry, good bugs, no caterpillars'), marmalade, Christmas tea, giant courgettes. One friend gives me 10 kilograms of freshly dug potatoes, which I carry home in a carrier bag slung over my handlebars. New rituals.

A neighbour invites me to a family lunch party on Christmas Eve. I take her a basket of plums and some sweet peas from the garden. She's lived here since 1974. She tells stories about the old villa that was removed from the section next door: the native trees along the driveway, the morepork that called at night, all gone now. I eat taro, cassava and raw fish in coconut for the first time. There's also chicken, ham, beef curry, potato and green salads and rice, then pavlova, washed down with wine and tea. Oof! I practically roll home.

'Goodbye darling,' she says, giving me a hug and kiss as I leave.

Christmas Day. Mum and my sisters have sent food parcels. I drink my homemade elderflower champagne with friends and eat the last Christmas puddings from my emergency stash.

On Boxing Day, I walk from the university's Orchard Road car park – no fruit trees in sight –to Turitea, south of the city. About a year ago, the council cut down the pines on one side of the walkway where it loops through a forest. For years I've come to this place to breathe out, think, and walk away my problems among the trees. I loved the dark-green shade, the calls of blackbirds and tūī, but now the trees are mulch on the walkway and many of the birds have gone. The treeless side of the route is hot, dusty and glaring. New houses are going in beyond the path; the forest echoes with drum'n'bass, hammering, builders' voices, power tools cutting through wood.

A woman with long faded-ginger hair and a floor-length patchwork skirt gathers pinecones from the fallen trees with her children. They speak an Eastern European language I can't identify. I imagine they could have stepped out of a European fairytale, but maybe I'm just being fanciful.

Another woman with long grey hair, more prosaically dressed in gum-boots, a dirty coat and pink rubber gloves, also picks up pinecones and wood from the debris.

'This is too good to leave here to rot,' she says. 'I'm collecting it for my pot-belly stove. It kept me warm all winter, but it's sad that they're gone.'

'Well, I guess people don't like the pines,' I say.

'What's wrong with them?! They support loads of life.'

Two well-groomed women wearing expensive exercise gear stop to see what's happening. We tell them about the trees being cut down.

'They're the wrong kind of trees,' says one.

When I get home, I ring a Polish friend who lives near the pine forest. I mention the tree removal, and she says she went to have a look after the trees were felled. 'It's so ugly,' she says. 'The trees were crying, weeping sap. I put my arms around them. And all the creatures that lived in there. Where will they go?'

People are divided on the question of exotic trees. While *Pinus radiata* is endangered in its native California, wilding pines are the number one weed pest in Aotearoa, spreading aggressively and damaging indigenous landscapes.[16] Some argue for total elimination, but others are more pragmatic, believing the pines aren't all bad. *Pinus radiata* suck up carbon faster than native trees, so the government is giving landowners subsidies to plant pines to meet climate change targets. While some owners reap the benefits of this carbon cash crop, others are culturally opposed to planting *radiata*.[17]

Research by ecologist Adam Forbes has shown that unharvested *radiata* plantations can nurse indigenous forest plants and support native bush regeneration. He argues that pine plantations are better than 'exotic pastoral landscapes' (that iconic Manawatū grassland).[18]

In a 2014 article in *New Zealand Geographic*, Kennedy Warne questioned whether we should distinguish between indigenous and exotic forest. He spoke to Matt McGlone, a palaeoecologist with Manaaki Whenua Landcare Research, and wrote:

> McGlone is adamant that we're going to have to get used to our forests sharing their space with exotic species. 'People love the tussock grasslands. I do, too. But they're recent, a human construction ... New Zealanders are particularly bad at this sort of ecological amnesia. They tend to think of their childhood recollection – the pohutukawa at the bach – as what is normative and what should be there in perpetuity.[19]

The Department of Conservation points out that wilding pines reduce grazing land; create fire risk; limit tourism and recreation activities; and use scarce water.[20] But grazing, fire, tourism/recreation and excessive water usage are human activities that damage the indigenous landscape. Humans brought the trees here, and the trees have done what was asked of them, putting down roots and thriving in their new home.

The issue pitches environmentalists against each other, just as wind farms do. Perhaps there's room for the exotic and the native in our landscape, both working together to fight climate change and orient us to our multicultural heritage.

The forest walkway won't stay bare for long – nature always finds a way. And the pine trees on the walkway will be replaced with native trees eventually. Jason told us in Memorial Park that the council is planting natives throughout the river corridor: it's called restorative distribution, 'So it doesn't look like "jolly old England".' The council gets complaints that natives are mundane, that people like exotic trees, but, he said, 'Once there's more of a native presence, we can put others in. Once the history's back in there the tension goes.'[21]

I understand why people want to get rid of the pine trees, but it doesn't stop me feeling sad that this cool, dark, quiet place I used to love, with its frisson of fairytale mystery, has gone. I recognise my sadness as homesickness, but it's more than that. It's the past that I've been longing for. The pine forests I grew up in are still there; it's my childhood that's gone, and I've been wallowing in pointless nostalgia.

The year is almost over. Discarded Christmas trees lie on grass berms, dropping brown needles, awaiting the rubbish collection.

New Year's Eve. I ring Mum to wish her a happy new year. Mum tells me that Nana brought her Orkney traditions with her when she moved south, continuing to celebrate Hogmanay, the Scottish new year celebration. It was more important to Nana than Christmas was.

'Mother always made someone come in over the threshold carrying a lump of coal at midnight: a dark-haired man, always.'

The preference for dark hair is thought to have come from the fear of blond strangers in a land much invaded by Vikings. Luckily, Grandad and my uncle were dark. The coal symbolised that there'd be enough fuel to warm the house for the year.

Talking to Mum makes me wonder whether Nana felt the same sense of dislocation that I do, both of us uprooting ourselves to move into a new landscape. Although Nana went a much shorter distance than me, she was effectively further away from her homeland. She went back to the Orkneys only once in the rest of her eighty-three years. The barriers I face to travelling are nothing compared to those she experienced.

I take heart, and make a new year's wish. Perhaps, next year, I will be able to see my family.

My tramping buddy drives me to Tōtara Reserve in Pohangina Valley, 40 kilometres out of the city. The reserve contains not just tōtara but kahikatea, black beech and rātā, ferns, shrubs and epiphytes. As we walk, we talk about how the pandemic is still bad in Europe: illness, deaths, restrictions and social division.

A massive tōtara towers over the rest of the forest. I hug it, but it would take four of me to encircle the whole trunk with my arms. My friend stands in a gap in the base of the tree and poses as I take a photo of her gazing up into the distant canopy.

'I'm glad I'm here now,' she says.

'Me too,' I reply.

# Weed

He prances barefoot across the lawn,
snatches the dandelion from its display case.
'Look,' he wants to say, 'Mummy, I found this choice
really weird thing in amongst all this grass, and it's yellow, it's
yellow.'
—JOHANNA AITCHISON, 'Miss Dust Lies on the Lawn with Lennox'[1]

**NEW YEAR.** A hush hangs over the city as people head to the beach
and bush to escape the heat. Not me. I'm still in Manawatū, working
and relishing the quiet.

The plums are finished. I throw nets over the pear and apple
trees, as far as I can reach, so that the garden looks haunted by a
shroud of Miss Haversham ghouls. The vegetable garden is as pretty
as a flower border, brimming over with pink- and yellow-stemmed
silverbeet, purple climbing beans twining up a bamboo tepee, green
and burgundy frilly lettuce edging the beds. Borage, with its tiny,
cucumber-flavoured mauve stars, pops up throughout the garden.

Oxalis, probably the most hated weed in New Zealand gardens,
has taken over the vegetable beds again. Oxalis was brought from
Europe as a pretty groundcover, but it's been too effective in covering
ground. I've been trying for years to eradicate it from my garden.
*Stuff* once ran an article called '9 ways to win the war on oxalis.'[2] I've
tried all nine suggestions, and now mainly do three: pull out its leaves
when they emerge, ignore it, or eat it. Oxalis is a member of the sorrel
family, and its citrusy leaves make zingy pesto. Its shamrock-shaped
leaves, long elegant stems and bright flowers are beautiful. In the
language of flowers, oxalis's relative, wood sorrel, symbolises joy.

I have dinner with my Polish friend. She shows me a package of mushrooms from her freezer, and says she picked them during lockdown. She was going to cook them tonight but thought I might not want to eat them.

I tell her about my fungi foraging, that I'm keen to try them, and she smiles.

'Next time I'll cook these!' she says.

As we eat the salmon she's cooked instead, my friend tells me she's been pulling old man's beard out of the university arboretum. 'These are *weeds*,' she says. Then she complains that her vegetable plot is full of oxalis.

I tell her about my new approach to the plant, and she says she'll give the pesto a go.

I look up 'weed' in the thesaurus. After all the drug-related words, it lists alien, foreign being, blow in, floater, immigrant, intruder, invader, outsider, refugee, stranger and noncitizen. But the thesaurus also gives less politically loaded synonyms: plant, flower, grass, seedling, shoot, tree, vine, herb and sprout. A weed is often defined simply as a plant in the wrong place. A weed might also be defined as a plant that affronts us by growing without our help.

A friend drops around and stops by the front border.

'What are these?' he asks, pointing to the orange California poppies. 'They're stunning.'

I promise him some seeds but warn him he'll have the poppies forever. When they first spread through the front garden, I kept pulling them out, because they messed with my carefully curated purple, white and red colour scheme. I tolerated orange only in the vegetable patch – in the marigolds that were growing there when I moved in and the nasturtiums that have now spread through the back garden. But I've let go now. So many plants won't grow in the hard clay – the ranunculus (my favourite flower) that I planted year after year, the gladioli that flopped and succumbed to rust, the lavender that went leggy and died – that I'm learning to embrace those that thrive without any effort from me. Plus, the orange is so exuberant, and I've come to love it against the purple. I wouldn't have thought of matching those colours, but together they sing.

The year has come to fruition. A blackbird patrols the berry patch like the strawberry thief in William Morris's famous textile design. The pear tree is weighed down with fruit. More blackbirds gorge themselves on the pears at the top of the tree that I couldn't reach with my nets. I think about getting the ladder so I can throw netting over the highest branches, but I decide against it; there's enough for me and the birds.

The apricot tree I put in five years ago is big but sparsely fruited. I tie hosiery cut-offs around each precious apricot: the birds aren't going to get those.

The seedlings of the decorative thistle echinops that I bought and planted and fussed over have died. But a huge purple thistle grows next to the roses. Every year I cut this thistle down, try to dig it out, but it keeps coming back. I decide to leave it (but to cut off the flowers before it sets seed) as a reminder of my Scotch ancestry. In this border, symbols of my heritage – English roses and Scottish thistles – grow side by side.

The histories of these introduced plants are entangled with our own. Scottish immigrants are thought to have brought thistles to New Zealand as potent reminders of their homeland. Like them and other migrants over the past 150 or so years, I built my garden in an attempt to recreate a lost pastoral, a landscape of the heart. But the plants that said home to them, and still do to me, can be a problem here (like the pines). Thistles have become pasture weeds, along with other plants imported for food, medicine, firewood, timber, aesthetic value or emotional support. Some species were carried to Aotearoa accidentally, mixed in with crop seeds or caught up in hay, straw or packing material. Not all introduced plants came with humans. Some arrived tucked between the feathers of migrating birds or were borne on the wind.[3]

Introduced species can lead to a boring homogenisation of the planet, a McDonald's flora and fauna that's the same everywhere you go. But this is happening because of us, our addiction to movement and power and consumer goods, which hastens climate change and snuffs out species. Manawatū is a monoculture of grass, supporting methane-belching cattle. Many of our gardens are also grass monocultures, dependent on fossil fuels and poison to conform to social niceties of manicured lawns and weed-free borders. The chemical-soaked landscapes we've created can't be any worse than nature left to its own devices.

Around the neighbourhood, purslane grows in the cracks of the footpath and spreads out across the tarmac. I first ate purslane in France, where it grew in a friend's garden. It's highly nutritious, full of iron, magnesium, potassium, manganese, vitamins and omega-3 fatty acids. It's lemony and crunchy too. I wish I could pick it, but the council sprays it with herbicide. Restricting plant growth to designated areas is the norm in most urban environments; any plant that spills over from its flower bed, planter or hanging basket is pounced upon and removed, usually with chemicals. The use of herbicide provides an illusion of control over nature, but the purslane keeps coming back. What do we fear will happen if we let this urban flora grow? Of course, some plants cause problems for humans and other species. But many of these wildings seem relatively harmless or even beneficial. As long as gutters and drains are kept clear, and footpaths don't become overgrown, what does a little untidiness matter? Urban plant growth increases biodiversity, feeds insects, reduces flood risk, absorbs pollution and reconnects citizens to the natural world. Plus, many of these plants were a valuable food source for the people who were here before us, and I can't help thinking we might need them again one day.

The *Guardian* reports on a new trend in England: 'rebel botanists' are chalking footpaths with the names of the plants growing through the cracks.[4] I'm surprised to read that chalking the pavement is illegal in Britain. Footpaths are routinely chalked in Aotearoa; during lockdown, messages of love and support appeared alongside hopscotch games, artworks and fitness routines. The article directs me to a UK project called More than Weeds, run by Sophie Leguil, who says that, during lockdown, people looked more closely at urban nature because they were forced to focus on what was close to them.

The More than Weeds website gives a history of weeding.[5] Humans ceased to be wanderers and became settlers with the invention of agriculture about 12,000 years ago. The minute humans stopped hunter-gathering and started farming, unwanted plants became a problem. Some people argue that agriculture itself created weeds: as the first farmers tilled or burnt the land, opportunist plants multiplied in the disturbed soil, reducing crop yields. Despite this, agriculture led to a human population boom. Mass migrations took settlers into new areas to cultivate crops and build homes. Migrants took domesticated wild plants with them, out of their natural environments where they grew in balance with other plants and animals, to new areas where they flourished unchecked.

When farmers became city-dwellers, wild plants growing without human permission were seen as a threat to civilisation and were manually removed by poor labourers. After the industrial revolution, highly toxic chemical weedkillers were developed. The chemical industry was boosted by World War I – sometimes described as the Chemists' War – as belligerent nations produced not only fuel and ammunition but also new chemical weapons, including the mustard gas my grandfather hallucinated about in his old age.

Food blockades meant that warring countries had to find new ways to feed their people, and industrial chemists turned their efforts to fertiliser to make farmland more productive. In World War II, British and American chemists worked on 2,4-Dichlorophenoxyacetic acid (2,4-D) as a potential weapon to destroy German and Japanese potato and rice crops, but the plants were resistant to the chemical. After the war, chemists turned their attention to the problem of scarce food supplies, and 2,4-D was used to kill broadleaf plants among cereal crops. The military language used against other nations was now transferred to unwanted plants (we still use it; for example, *Stuff*'s 'war on oxalis'). As prosperity returned, the herbicide found a new application killing plants – particularly dandelions – in lawns.

In the early 1970s, agricultural biotechnology corporation Monsanto developed glyphosate, and began marketing it as Roundup. Glyphosate is now the most widely used herbicide in the world. In the US, glyphosate has been used to kill milkweed, the food source of monarch butterflies. It's thought this has contributed to the 81 percent decline in the butterflies' numbers. Debate about the effects of glyphosate on human, animal and soil health rumbles on. Since 2014, many countries have banned or restricted its use, although it's still allowed in Aotearoa. Plants are starting to fight back too: here, creeping oxalis (a native variety), nodding thistle and giant buttercup have evolved resistance to 2,4-D. With climate change, these plants will extend their range across the country.[6]

Leguil asks why, when we talk a lot about rewilding the countryside, we don't also talk about rewilding our cities, and says, 'spontaneous flora may be a first step needed to heal our broken relationship with nature.'[7]

Through the window I see a pair of little rosy-headed finches pecking around in the lawn. I go out to the garage, extract a small green plastic bottle of Roundup, pour the remnants into some rubble under the deck, and put the bottle in the recycling.

It's been hot and dry for a couple of weeks. The lawn stops growing in the heat, but dandelions thrive, opening up their faces to the sun and brightening the garden with their ray-of-sunshine petals. I've heard dandelions referred to as 'DYCs' or 'damned yellow composites' – defined by Wikipedia as 'any of the numerous species of composite flowers that have yellow flowers and can be difficult to tell apart … sometimes reserved for those yellow composites of no particular interest.'[8] Plants 'of no particular interest' include chamomile, sow thistle, chicory, fleabane and hawkweed. These flowers, from the Asteraceae family (which includes sunflowers, daisies and echinops), can be invasive outside their natural territory but also provide pollinators with food.[9]

The *Guardian*'s rebel botanists article also reports research that found that many urban weeds provide more and better pollen and nectar than garden plants. The most valuable pollinator plants are 'dandelions and their lookalikes' – the damned yellow composites, those plants of no particular interest.[10]

I decide to stop mowing the front garden, to leave the DYCs, and create a wild area as a haven for insects.

In 2019 the UN warned that nearly half of insect pollinators, particularly bees and butterflies, risk global extinction.[11] The ubiquitous dandelion, the flower that turns into a clock, counts down the hours.

I go to an online writing workshop and try to argue that weeds have some redeeming features. Someone says I sound like a butt-ignorant, whingeing Pom.

She emails me afterwards to apologise, and says she spends hours pulling out gorse. I tell her I understand; that my sister does the same with rhododendrons in her local wood in England. I hate upsetting people, and even though I've been a New Zealand citizen for seventeen years and have a black-and-silver passport, I still don't feel like a 'proper' Kiwi. I drink tea not coffee, I love gooseberries and hate feijoas, I don't have a car and I think rugby's boring. I'm still a foreigner, so maybe I should keep my mouth shut. But the rhododendrons and gorse keep growing back, and I can't help wondering if there's a better way to spend time and money.

Later, the workshop leader says, 'It was interesting how the other students thought you were quite eccentric.'

I am a foreign being, an immigrant, an outsider. Maybe this is why I ally myself with those plants that know how it feels to be an alien.

The campus gardens, usually so carefully tended by groundskeepers, are a crazy, mixed-up, exuberant jungle of roses, hydrangeas, lilies, tropical flowers I can't identify, and opportunist plants making the most of their reprieve from hoes and sprays. I sit for a while, listening to the cicadas, watching a damselfly zip about, and inhaling the scent of a thousand blooms.

I walk down to my friend's commemorative maple tree. The maple is not quite big enough to hug yet, but I touch its bark, then put my hand on the plaque. The metal is warm, reflecting the heat of the sun, and a reminder of my friend's warmth. When I feel self-doubt, I go there and talk to her. She always tells me, 'F.E.A. Fuck 'em all. Put on your big girl pants and give 'em hell, baby.'

I watch a recording of a political ecology conference hosted by a research group at the university. British scientist Fred Pearce, author of a book called *The New Wild*, and environmental correspondent for *New Scientist*, is advocating for weeds. I wait for someone to call him a butt-ignorant, whingeing Pom, but no one does.

A man posts in the comments: 'We are at war here (I am sure you have read the propaganda) and to oppose it feels like treason. Your new wild does exist here, however, and is flourishing where it can. So the war goes on ... and we hide.'[12]

So, I'm not alone. I feel as though, in the war on nature, I've found the resistance.

I water the garden every morning, and by lunchtime the soil is dry again. Radishes, parsnips and beetroot, which need to penetrate the hard clay soil to form large roots, turn spindly and bolt prematurely to seed. This is the busiest time of year for gardeners. I shovel compost from the heap to the vegetable beds, then sow more radishes. I plant squash and three kinds of basil – the traditional Genovese pesto herb, an aniseed-flavoured purple type, and a lemon variety – to eat with the tomatoes when they're ripe. Curly, dark-green parsley grows everywhere: handfuls go into pasta sauce for an iron boost. Monarch butterflies float around, as big as small birds, alighting on scarlet runner bean flowers, white agapanthus and red pineapple sage blooms to suck out nectar.

The garden is tipped on the edge of descent from the perfection of early summer into exuberant chaos. 'Drunken Woman' lettuce sprawls in the beds. A greenfinch with yellow-barred wings swings on a borage plant, pecking at the seeds. Rust creeps across the broad bean plants and mint, covering the leaves with dusty orange pustules. I pull out the spent plants and throw them in the corner of the garden.

There have never been so many pears. Tomorrow, if it's cooler, I'll ride round the neighbourhood and drop some off to friends and put a bagful in the pātaka kai.

A sudden downpour in the afternoon freshens the air. The rain is a relief. I walk on the field and get soaked through my raincoat. It feels deliciously cool after the heat of high summer.

Hail turning to heavy rain. Sunflowers sag under the weight of the summer storm. When the rain stops, I go out to the garden. The hedge quakes with tiny birds that fill the air with twittering. Fragrant white jasmine grows determinedly upwards up through the hedge. A bedraggled waxeye in the apricot tree doesn't move as I approach. Now the ground has softened, I dig a fork into the flooded grass and vegetable beds to create drainage in the clay. Tomatoes swell. The green plum tree has put on its autumn coat, and a strong wind blows leaves all over the garden.

In the evening, rain hammers on the roof. It's cold enough to need socks and to wrap myself in a throw; it's blissful.

Cicadas shrill after the rain. A blackbird hops past the window with a big chunk of apricot in its beak. I go outside, where debris from the storm litters the ground. The birds have foiled my apricot-protection device, managing to peck through the hosiery. I salvage as much fruit as I can, cutting out the bits the birds have pecked. The blackbirds have also successfully navigated two layers of netting to eat the apples. My relationship with the birds is sorely tested.

My Polish friend comes around to get grapefruit. She tells me her husband had weeded the garden without her knowing.

'I tried to make oxalis pesto. But I didn't have enough oxalis! Who would think I could ever say this?'

The garden starts to wrap up for the year. Flowers bow down, gathering energy before a final fling when they'll distribute their seeds out to the universe. I pick sweet-pea pods to save seed for next year, and leave them in a bowl on the kitchen table to dry out. Occasionally I hear a crack as a pod opens and catapults seed across the room. The plant does this by drying one side of the seedcase more slowly than the other, causing it to twist as it opens.

By the back fence, a karaka tree is covered in clusters of sweet-smelling orange fruit. Seedlings sprout in the grass around the tree. I decide to leave them, to form my own karaka grove. Karaka are considered weedy in some parts of the country: yesterday's hallowed plant is today's weed.[13]

For my wild area, I'd envisaged a wildflower-studded meadow with long grasses waving in the breeze. There are grasses, from which finches eat seeds, but the only flower so far is another stately thistle, taller than me, that has erupted into purple-tufted blooms. The bees seem to love it. I consider my options for cutting a path through the grass if I turn the whole lawn over to wildlife: a non-motorised push mower, a scythe?

The toddler next door is peeking through the hedge, saying something to me that I can't make out. His mum comes over and translates: he's saying 'Mower, mower.' She tells me he's obsessed with lawnmowers. 'I have to carry him on my back when I mow the lawn,' she says.

It's hot, and dry. I walk across the field, through the school gate and up the pathway to the terrace above. I look down over the graffitied, corrugated-metal fence, out across the field to the ranges. Summer turns the world brown and blond. A bird flies out of the tall grass on the side of the pathway with a cicada in its beak.

'It's got long, hasn't it?' says a woman coming down the path.

'Yes,' I say, and 'Isn't it beautiful?' I think.

I walk round the block. A man daubs weedkiller onto a dandelion with a paintbrush. Another man smokes while cutting his berm with a ride-on. The combination of cigarettes and cut grass is a heady mix that reminds me of Dad. At weekends when I was a child, he mowed the lawn of an elderly woman who lived in an old, rambling house with a huge garden full of mature trees. I used to go with him and rake up the grass cuttings, for which he paid me 20p. My first job.

It's Saturday, and half the neighbourhood seems to be out with their lawnmowers. The city is getting a haircut. Except one property, where the berm is unmown, the lawn bright with dandelions, the borders full of tradescantia and oxalis. Toys lie about the garden, and children's clothes hang to dry on the veranda. The untidy house is at risk of social judgement. I think about my wild lawn and fear that if I stop mowing I'll be judged too; that my long grass and wildflowers will be considered an inability to cope rather than a conscious decision to let go of tidiness. The drone of lawnmowers and other power tools is the soundtrack to a sunny weekend, the diligent homeowners' warm-weather ritual.

I walk on past an abandoned building site that has bloomed into a tiny meadow of daisies, clover, dandelions, chamomile and vetch. The wind ripples through the long, tawny grass. Next door, a woman kneels on a border of bare soil, hand-weeding between evenly spaced small shrubs. Where did this idea come from, that gardens have to be manicured; that an untidy garden reflects an untidy mind? Pesticides and herbicides have made the world neat but sterile, like a Botoxed face. The building-site meadow lifts my spirits: it comforts me to know that after we've concreted over the last patch of soil, and when humans are gone from this Earth, a weed will break through the tarmac, and nature will reestablish itself in some old and familiar, then new and amazing forms.

A tagger has spray-painted electricity boxes and walls around the neighbourhood; his signature is a male face with wavy hair and beard. I imagine him as a pagan green man.

Back on my street, I peer through a gate at a luscious flower garden. The borders billow with David Austin roses, lilies, delphiniums, echinacea and lavender. A classic English cottage garden. The owner is there, so I stop to chat, tell him I think his garden is the most beautiful on the street, maybe in the city. He denies it, then invites me in for a mini guided tour and introduces himself; he has the same name as my first serious boyfriend, whom I met at university.

He points to a lavender bush: 'This one's Munstead.'

I know he'll understand, so I tell him that for the first year of my life I lived on Munstead Lane, just up the road from the home of famous English plantswoman and garden designer Gertrude Jekyll, who pioneered the naturalistic planting style. Maybe there was no escaping being a gardener for me. Dad bought the run-down house cheaply and was doing it up until his back problem became too much. Mum recalls walking down the lane with my two-year-old brother and one-year-old sister, pregnant with me, to get the bus to the phone box to call the chiropractor, while Dad lay in agony on the hallway floor.

'Gertrude Jekyll? Well, I can't believe it!' my neighbour says. 'I must come and look at your garden.'

Despite myself, I feel embarrassed at the thought of him seeing my long grass, so tell him about my insect haven idea.

'You're doing the right thing,' he says.

His flower garden began as an extravagantly romantic gesture. He created it because his wife hated him mowing the daisies and dandelions in the lawn.

After university I moved into a rented cottage with my boyfriend. I grew sunflowers by the front door, but I wasn't a gardener yet, although I loved flowers. I had a new job in the city, and every day I took the bus along a winding lane up to a high ridge that looked out over a meadow bright with wildflowers. The meadow reflected back through the bus window the joy I felt as I stepped into adulthood.

In autumn, signs went up: the wildflower meadow was going to be destroyed to make way for an executive housing development. I cried on the bus when the diggers moved in.

My boyfriend and I argued at a party. He took off, and a friend drove me home. My boyfriend crept in at six, stood in the bedroom doorway.

'I'm sorry,' he said.

'Where have you been?'

He looked down. I noticed his bloodied knuckles.

'What happened?'

'I smashed up the diggers that were destroying your flower meadow.'

This was my first taste of environmental activism. And still the most extravagantly romantic gesture anyone has ever made for me.

Heather gave me wildflower bombs for Christmas. As I sprinkle them over the front border, I reflect on how military language is now being used by the resistance too.

Accepting weeds in the garden is my way of relinquishing the fight to control nature, a battle I'll never win. I've tried to garden this patch of earth, but it reverts to wildness so quickly. I used to get stressed about it, but now I see it as a life-affirming sign that nature is kicking back. I'm leaving an ecosystem to evolve that supports everything that lives here, rather than taking a military approach to eradicating plants that aren't really a problem.

I ride to the army camp and stop at the end of the path. As I'm standing there chugging water, a man gets out of an SUV and looks over, so I say hello. He looks official, so I ask if he works for the council.

'Yes, I look after all the plants along here.'

I ask him about the new plantings going in along the path, and he points out across the gully and says, 'We go in there and collect seed from the native plants; it gets planted, then gets put back in the bush.' He points down over the gully again. 'See that tree lucerne? That's not a native but we leave it in because the birds like it. It's their only food source at this time of year. That tree will be full of wood pigeons.'

I mention that there's a patch of non-native wildflowers further down the path, with a sign asking people not to pick the flowers because they provide food for native birds. He looks dubious.

'As long as it's not pink mallow, I'm forever ripping that out.'

I tell him about the conference; that some argue it's natural for plants and animals to come on the wind and waves and be naturally incorporated into the landscape.

'Not if I can help it!' he says.

I tell him about the villa next door to me being removed, the native trees being cut down, and how I went to the council and was told by a man in a grey suit that it was progress.

'Fuck progress,' he says, but then adds, 'Well, everyone wants new houses.'

'Not everyone. Not weirdos like me.'

'I didn't mean you were a weirdo.'

'No, it's okay, I know I'm a weirdo. I'm a proud weirdo.' I smile and get back on my bike.

'You're a good sort. We'll be working here for a while; come and say hello.'

The man smiles too, and as I ride away I feel that, maybe, I belong.

# Insect

And shrill cicada, far and near
Piped on his high exultant third.
Summer! Summer! he seems to say—
Summer! He knows no other word.

—ANNE GLENNY WILSON, 'A Spring Afternoon in New Zealand'[1]

**IN THE GARDEN A CENTIPEDE** scuttles up a flax flower, caterpillars carve white channels into brassicas, and a bright green praying mantis like a small alien turns its head on a rose bush. I throw net curtains over the cabbages to keep the white butterflies off. They can have the nasturtiums.

I'm reading about insect Armageddon. The phrase came into use after a 2017 study found a 75 percent decline in flying insects over twenty-seven years in German nature reserves.[2] Nature reserves! Where those very creatures should be abundant. As I read, I hear a gentle tapping on the window: a large moth is attracted to my light.

I used to live in the country and on the dark nights a natural history documentary played on the curtainless kitchen window: moths sat on the glass, their underwings shades of chocolate, silver and honeycomb, scalloped, marbled and burnished. The first summer after I moved into my current home in town seven years ago, I considered insect screens for the windows. But in the second year I noticed fewer insects coming into the house, and since then I've barely even thought about insects. One or two come in, but not enough to bother me. The majority just seem to have disappeared.

During my childhood, every (infrequent) night-time car journey meant insects coating the windscreen and headlights. The reduction in insects splattered on cars even has a name: the windshield phenomenon.

Cicadas rasp and buzz in the garden.

I give the house a (late) new year clean but feel bad dusting down the cobwebs. The spiders scuttle away, and I'm careful not to pick them up on the duster, even though I know they'll spin more webs.

My friend Kerstin is learning to keep bees, so we go to Feilding to meet mother-and-daughter beekeepers Jen and Penny.

As I get out of the car, I hear an angry buzzing sound: motorbikes racing around the track at the local stadium. Penny comes out to greet us, then leads us into the house to meet her quiet husband, Mike. Jen is there too; she works for a commercial beekeeper and wears a tee-shirt with a bee design and a tiny silver bee pendant.

Today Penny is doing the annual honey harvest from her hobby hives. She opens the hives only during the day, while the female forager bees are out gathering pollen, and explains that, on a sunny day like this, the bees work from sunrise to sunset. We make inevitable jokes: the females work while the male drones live in the hive, eating and shagging. The women roll their eyes. Mike smiles and says nothing.

Penny tells us that the queen mates with as many drones as possible and can lay fifteen hundred eggs a day. Once the drones have served their reproductive purpose, the other bees drive them out of the hive.

'Then what happens to them?' I ask.

'You don't want to know,' says Jen.

'They die,' says Penny.

Penny, Kerstin and I go into the garden, where they don white beekeeping suits. Honeybees buzz around fruit trees, and a tūī sups honey water from a feeder. Penny warns Kerstin not to lean forward as the bees will sense the heat of her nose and sting her.

She says, 'These suits say they're sting-proof but they're not. I've learnt the hard way. But the last thing a bee wants is to sting you, because they die.' She tells us that only females sting; their stinger has a barb that pulls their guts out if they use it.

I sit nearby while Penny extracts wooden frames filled with honeycomb from the hives, gently removing bees with a soft brush before handing the frames to Kerstin to put in a box. Penny explains that at this time of year, heading into autumn, the bees' pātaka are well stocked, ready for the cold weather to come.

When the box is full, Penny and Kerstin carry it into the house. Penny cuts through the wax cell caps, then uses a manual press to squeeze the honeycomb through muslin. Amber honey pours out through a tap into a bucket, then Penny puts it into jars.

She says, 'I don't like honey, can't stand the stuff. I just like bees.' She hands us both a jar and says, 'This is unprocessed: look out for bee bums and legs.'

'From bees that have died of natural causes?' I ask hopefully.

'Or been caught in the frames and gone to their sweet sticky deaths,' Penny replies.

Jen is setting up a queen bee breeding business. Queens live for about nine years, but in commercial operations they're replaced every year.

'What do they do with the old ones? Release them into the wild?' I ask, slightly less hopefully.

'Yes, they might find a colony without a queen. But they often die.'

Jen explains that a swarm occurs when there are enough bees to form a new colony and the queen takes off to find a home. If a hive is left with no queen, the workers feed a selection of cells that become queen cells. If one queen comes out before the others, she stings her rivals to death before they can emerge. Queens don't die if they sting because they don't have the fatal barb. If several queens emerge, they fight to the death until there's only one left.

'Sounds like *The Hunger Games*,' I say.

Jen melts combs in the slow cooker. She doesn't like honey much either. I'm not a big honey fan, but she says it's completely different from the supermarket stuff and offers me a taste. I scoop it up with a finger. The wax is creamy, with the texture of chewing gum. The dark, rich brown honey is fruity and more complex than I expected.

A big red kettle boils on the hob. Penny makes tea and gets a cake out of a pan. We sit outside and eat gingerbread. She tells us that if you want hives in your garden, you need your neighbours' permission.

I say, 'I live by a school so they probably wouldn't agree. I just want pollinators.'

'What about bumblebees?' asks Kerstin. 'Don't they live underground?'

'Yes, they do,' says Penny, 'but bumblebees bite through the back of flowers to get the nectar. They ate all my bean flowers.'

'Bees or beans? It's like fruit or birdsong,' I say.

Mike nods. He's just netted the entire vegetable garden. I ask if they have many birds here, and Penny says they hear a morepork at night; it keeps them awake sometimes. I think I would deliberately stay awake to hear one. She says, 'The tūī fight; they're territorial. There were nine in the garden, and they bullied a smaller one to death. Right now, they're pushing the babies out of the nest.'

The bees are also under assault. Jen says that bees from another hive will steal honey if resources are scarce. Wasps attack bees, too, but not for the honey: they're carnivores and are after the larvae. They also bite bees' heads off and eat the bodies. Then there's varroa mite, which sucks lipids out of the bee's body. Jen says the varroa mite is like having a bug stuck to your body – except that for a bee a varroa mite is soccer-ball-sized. It doesn't sound easy, being a bee.

We get on to the subject of insect Armageddon, and I talk about the insect haven I'm hoping to create in my garden. Penny has left dead trees as a wētā habitat; Jen's stopped mowing her lawn and now, she says, it's full of insects.

After Kerstin drops me off, I read about the history of honeybees in Aotearoa. The delightfully named Englishwoman Mary Bumby is thought to have introduced honeybees in 1839 when she came to Hokianga as housekeeper to her brother John, a Methodist missionary. John liked honey, so Mary brought two hives on the sea voyage. The bees inevitably went forth and multiplied, establishing wild colonies in the bush.[3]

Bumblebees were introduced in 1885 to pollinate new plants brought by colonists. A 2006 University of California Berkeley study found that 35 percent of the world's food crops are pollinated by animals. But pollinators are threatened by pesticides, herbicides, pathogens, introduced species and habitat loss. Study co-author Claire Kremen argues for the benefits of more sustainable farming practices, such as leaving weeds and native plants to grow alongside introduced crops.[4]

I decide to stop mowing the lawn altogether, for the insects. Perhaps it will increase my harvest too.


The fresh, bright summer garden ebbs into faded beauty. Plump cobalt-blue hydrangeas morph into antique shades of burgundy, mauve, violet, pink.

Tomatoes ripen: egg-shaped, round, fluted, large, small, red, green, maroon. This is the moment I've been waiting for. An earwig scurries along the netting as I harvest. I pick beans, too, heritage varieties given to me by a Californian friend, with names redolent of Native American tribes – 'Blue Lake', 'Turkey Craw', 'Flagg', 'Yoeme Purple', 'Hidatsa Shield'. I leave some beans to dry on the plant to add to my winter food supplies.

The air vibrates with the cicadas' summer chorus.

It's so hot. Sweat beads between my eyelashes. I sit in cool lavender-scented baths, drink litres of elderflower cordial, eat frozen yogurt, pull the curtains against the heat.

I talk to Karen on WhatsApp. It's snowing in Oxford, and she's made snowwomen in masks as lockdown entertainment. One lies on a sun lounger, in a bikini.

'That one's you,' she says, 'because it's summer there.'

Imagining myself as a snowwoman helps me cool down.

This evening I stand on the street chatting to my neighbour. We talk about the cicadas, how loud they are this year, how there seem to be more of them. I hope so. I tell her about my plan to let the grass grow long to encourage insects.

'As long as it's the good insects and not the bad ones,' she says.

'Hopefully they'll balance out,' I say.

I feel midges biting my bare legs, bid my neighbour goodnight and go inside. I'll need to work on my sales pitch for fighting insect Armageddon.

I sit by the french windows to read. A few unidentified insects fly in: a large buff-coloured moth; a black-and-white-and-red chequered flying bug. A tiny ghost-like damselfly that I saw on the window earlier now crawls down my top. Good insects or bad? So many creatures, I couldn't begin to name them, and we're slowly killing them all.

In the market gardens, a figure in a grey boiler suit, peaked hat and gumboots walks slowly, holding a sprayer. It's hot, dry and dusty. A truck from the gravel pit blows grit into my face as I ride. Three cows lie down in a field, but no rain is due for a week. Fields of corn taller than me. Yellow hot pokers glow in the berms.

Along the river path, clouds of tiny black flies flit around my mouth and nose, catch in my hair, land on my lips and eyes. Once this would have bothered me, but now it makes me glad there are still some insects left. If I create an insect haven in the garden, does that offset the bugs I kill while travelling, like a form of carbon credit? This makes me wonder whether the increase in traffic since my childhood has also contributed to insects' decline, not just by roads taking their territory, and lights affecting their behaviour, but also because so many are being squashed against windscreens.

Dogs cool off in the river where the water level is low. On the way home the cows have abandoned hope of rain and are on their feet again.

While I'm preparing rhubarb from the garden for dinner, an ant and an iridescent green beetle wander about the benchtop. I shepherd them on to a bit of rhubarb leaf, then carry them outside.

Later, I'm too hot and tired to do anything other than lie on the sofa and watch TV. An advert for fly spray guarantees to kill all insects. I turn the TV off. Extermination of insects to protect food crops or prevent disease is one thing, but killing creatures that don't pose any threat to us is another.

As I sit on the steps of the porch this morning to put on my shoes, I notice I'm on an ant motorway. Yesterday I left a container of pear peelings outside the door to take to the compost. A long trail of ants marches from inside the pot, across the porch and down a crack at the top of the steps. I carry the pot to the compost pile, taking some ants with it, and wonder what ants do when they're moved into a new environment. I know there's an ant colony at the back of the garden; they regularly march with what looks like single-minded, single-file purpose across the back gate. That purpose is to break down organic matter, return nutrients to the earth and aerate the soil.

I'm busy too, making preserves from my garden supply of pears and the fruit gathered on foraging expeditions. Sweat pops out on my face and back as the saucepans bubble, but my pātaka must be filled for winter. By the end of the afternoon, the shelves are stacked with jars.

A spider hanging from a web casts a shadow on the window frame above my nature collection. I leave the spider, and its web, there. The house and garden have become a shared space.

On the field, the elder tree's leaves turn gold as the berries ripen into glistening black jet beads. My cousin in London sends me a recipe for elderberry tincture to ward off viruses, so I pick bunches of berries. Something large and white in the grass catches my eye. Is it a puffball already? No – it's a half-deflated soccer ball. But small, brown-scaled puffballs are popping up in the grass, and boletes too.

The garden slumps. Plants wilt in the midday sun. Sunflowers hang their heads, heavy with seed; I leave them in the ground as a food source for the birds come winter. The rain that's been forecast but not arrived for three days is so close I can smell it. Corn ripens; squashes sprawl across the garden, escaping their enclosure. Aphids coat the leaves of the orange and grapefruit trees. Mosquitoes hatch on the old metal bath that holds rainwater. I hope they don't migrate into my neighbour's garden.

Robert Billens' 1937 souvenir booklet of Palmerston North's diamond jubilee tells of 'the tribulations of the pioneers at the hands of the mosquito'. Swampy Manawatū was a breeding ground for the insects, which plagued the colonists. Billens also recounts the apocryphal tale of 'the fat stock buyer who lost fifty bullocks but found millions of mosquitoes on the top rail of the fence picking their teeth with the horns'.[5]

Picking peaches this evening, mosquitoes mob my legs. I slap at them with my hands, but I can already feel the tingling of bites.

Lying in bed I hear two differently pitched mosquito whines. I switch on the light and squash a couple of insects that may or not be the offending mozzies, leaving a dark smear on the cream paint of the wall and a black mark on my conscience.

In the morning, my legs are a dot to dot of red blotches.

My tolerant attitude towards ants has almost literally come back to bite me in the arse. Columns of ants march through the pantry and laundry. There are ants in the cupboard, ants in the microwave, ants in the teapot.

I squash them and hope they might go away, but over the next couple of days they spread through the house. I spot an ant floating in my bath and another in my bed (these are the ones that might bite me). I get ant bait from the supermarket.

'We have a lot of ants too,' says a workmate. 'We put the jam and honey in the fridge,' she continues, trying to be helpful.

'That would be okay if there weren't also ants in my fridge,' I say.

I message Karen: 'I have new pets! Ants. Yay.'

She writes back: 'Used powder on last summer's ant onslaught but it was windy and I ended up in A and E after inhaling it. Had ant man round. He'd never seen ants marching in quite the way they were doing ... lines of them going up into my garage roof, to store food in between the breeze block walls.'

This morning, the splashback behind the kitchen sink is covered in ants. The moving black mass makes me feel slightly hysterical. I take some deep breaths and wipe them away with tissues. After finding ants in sealed jars of homemade jam and chutney in the pantry, I reluctantly call a pest control company. A man comes three days later.

He says, 'This is really bad. There must be a huge nest underneath your house.'

The man installs plastic feeding trays which say 'Extermination Café' on the side. He tells me the ants will come for the bait: 'It's like heroin to them.' I think about how the colony has probably been there for longer than my house has been. I feel bad about poisoning the ants, and hope they go out on a drug-induced high. After a few days, the marching ants have gone from the kitchen, and the outside step is covered with ant corpses, like a battlefield. I feel like a hypocrite.

I see a green praying mantis through the quadra glass of the bathroom window. I wonder if it can see me too and, if it can, what do I look like, and is it judging me?

We're approaching that edge time, when the seasons blur; cold in the mornings but hot during the day. I go for a long walk to the place where golden peaches roll down the bank and wild damsons grow. Fork-tailed swifts swoop around me, casting grey shadows on the concrete path. The fields are straw-coloured, a muted late-summer landscape. A damselfly helicopters over a pond. I continue walking alongside a flower meadow that looks like the one I'm hoping for in my garden. Bulls in a field swish away insects with their tails, their muscles twitching where flies sit on their flanks. I'm not sleeping well because of the heat. Like the garden, I'm running out of steam as it gets hotter and hotter. My tee-shirt is wet beneath my backpack. Halfway around my loop walk, I just have to sit down. Cicadas make their slow *click – click – buzz*. It's a lazy sound that makes me want to sleep. I close my eyes and am thinking about lying down for a snooze when I hear footsteps behind me. A jogger.

'Did you run out of oomph?' she asks.
'I'm afraid I did,' I say.

The forecast rain has passed over without falling on Manawatū. I water the garden in the morning. At lunchtime I go for a walk, but it's so hot I don't stay out for long. Down the street a man in shorts and white vest pours water from a kettle onto the footpath.

'Well, how about that,' he says as I pass. 'I'm just killing the ants.'

Into Memorial Park where a man in an orange fluoro vest sprays weeds. A jogger stops at the bottom of the steps to get his breath back. The frogs are quiet. Maybe they've had enough of the heat too.

Back home, a cicada screams in my ear as I walk past the rambling rose on the trellis.

Good insects: bees on the fennel flowers; dramatic monarchs; dainty red, black and yellow butterflies on the roses. Bad insects: mosquitoes biting my legs; wasps that eat bees; aphids smothering the citrus trees; white butterflies destroying the cabbages. This is an anthropocentric view, of course. But even those insects we don't like serve multiple functions in our ecosystem, providing sustenance for other creatures such as birds and fish, recycling organic material, building soil, pollinating plants.

Sitting reading by the window, I'm distracted by a spider as she approaches a fly caught in her web. She methodically consumes her prey; it's a horror show, but it's compelling viewing. This is the food chain and no different from what we do. What will the spider eat if we kill all the insects?

I learn another term, 'trophic cascade', which means the addition or removal of predators and/or prey from an ecosystem, leading to catastrophic changes in the food web.

This landscape buzzes with innumerable lives, human and non-human. The consequences of our actions are continuously felt, and will be felt into the future. We are all related: to each other, and to the creatures that surround and support us. If we destroy those creatures, we also destroy ourselves.

The trunks of the fruit trees are studded with cast-off cicada shells.

Cicadas start their lives as eggs on vegetation. After hatching, the nymphs burrow underground and spend up to five years in subterranean chambers, living on sap from tree roots. The nymphs shed their skins several times as they grow. As they approach adulthood, the juveniles dig their way to the surface. When the nymphs are ready to leave the soil, they emerge at night and climb up trees, lodging on the trunks. Here the nymphs moult for the final time, cracking open their skins, breaking out of their chrysalises and shaking loose their wings. By morning, the cicadas' wings are dry, and the transformation from dull, brown ground-dweller to dazzling flying insect is complete. The cicadas fly away to spend a few glorious weeks singing in the sunshine, mating, feeding on sap and laying eggs before their brief adult lives are over.[6]

The human life span is the reverse of the cicada life cycle: childhood is brief, and adulthood long (if you're lucky). But time and perception stretch and warp: childhood seems to last forever when you're in it, and adult life passes quickly. In the same way, the first few weeks of lockdown, which I spent immersed in the soil, seemed long and slow. But time has disappeared so fast since then.

Today there are more Covid cases in Aotearoa. In the UK, the virus has mutated, but Mum has been vaccinated and I feel reassured. The time before Covid feels so long ago. When the problems of the world seem overwhelming, memories become places of sanctuary. But insects don't look back. Their transformation is their strength. The cicadas fall silent. There's a perceptible shift in the air: summer is nearly over. Yellow leaves drift from the plum tree in the light breeze to form a layer of mulch. I scatter wildflower seeds – no more careful colour schemes. Mushrooms pop up in what was lawn. I pick the last tomatoes to ripen on the windowsill, clear vegetable beds of beanstalks and prepare the soil for next year's crops, ready to start the cycle all over again.

# Epilogue

Still there are seasons, summers, migrations,
Flowerings and rebirths
—CHARLES DOYLE, 'Starlings and History'[1]

THIS YEAR HAS TRANSFORMED MY WORLD. Life is movement, but Covid forced me to pause. I'd never considered myself part of nature – never, really, stopped to consider myself at all; I was too busy moving forwards, or sideways, or backwards, rather than just stopping and looking at where I was *now*.

And once I stopped, the past reappeared and everything began to fall into place. I understand my parents' lives now; in some ways I'm repeating them. I'm becoming more and more like Mum; our similarity is a comforting reminder of the circularity of life. I share her love of gardening, birds, history – and travel.

But everything has changed: I feel uncomfortable about travelling, because of Covid, but also because of the carbon cost of the flight. Heather comes to my rescue once again when she tells me about the concept of love miles: it's okay to travel to see family. Mum is thinking of moving into a retirement village, but not until she's seen the roses bloom in her garden one more time. She rarely complains, so when she tells me she's having trouble coping, I know it's time to go home.

The godwits are leaving too. And I know, like them, I'll be coming back. The birds belong to two places, and so do I.

Sitting under a tree on campus in the early autumn sun, I feel the hard, chunky bark and the strength of the trunk against my back. The landscape looks brown and grey, but as my eyes slowly attune to the scene I see that the drabness is deceptive: this patch is multi-layered and textured, pulsing with life. Amber sap oozes from the tree. A fly buzzes around small animal droppings. Around me lie mottled mushrooms, rounded stones, sculptural seed cases, lumpy tree roots, discarded cicada shells, and dried pinecones and needles. Then my eye picks out spiders' webs strung low across the ground, glinting in the sunlight.

Soil, fungi, fruit, water, star, stone, blossom, bird, wind, tree, weed, insect, human: I see how everything is linked in a shimmering net of connection, and I feel my heart beat.

# Acknowledgements

I begin by acknowledging and paying my respects to the cultural, spiritual, historical and traditional associations of Rangitāne o Manawatū as mana whenua and kaitiaki of this region.

Grateful acknowledgements also go to everyone who helped me to write this book:

My family for allowing me to use our shared history, especially Mum, in whose company I enjoyed walking down Memory Lane.

Karen and Heather, my lockdown rocks.

Everyone who supported me during lockdown, especially Wayne, Josie, Charlotte, Mani, Kate and Hayden, Kerstin, Lynne, my workmates and neighbours. There were others, too numerous to list here, and I'm grateful for their support.

My Master of Creative Writing supervisor Ingrid Horrocks, for her tactful guidance and encouragement while I was writing this manuscript, and my study buddies at Massey University, especially Helen and Jo.

The Earle Creativity Trust, Laura Watts and Write Across New Zealand for financial support and self-belief.

Sue Wootton and her team at Otago University Press, who have been a dream to work with.

My editor Jane Parkin whose skilful polishing has made this book as good as it could be.

Almost everyone I encountered while writing this narrative; all are present in the story, whether named or not.

The publishers, agents, writers and their estates who gave me permission to quote from copyright material.

Quotation from 'Waiariki' in *Selected Stories* by Patricia Grace, © 1991 Penguin, used by permission of Patricia Grace and Penguin; quotation from 'The New Loaf' in *An Open Book* by David Malouf, © 2018 University of Queensland Press, used by permission of David Malouf and University of Queensland Press; quotation from 'Mushrooms' in *Canterbury and Other Poems* by Basil Dowling, © 1949 The Caxton Press, used by permission of Virginia Strauss, Imogen Jasch and The Caxton Press; quotation from 'Peach, the Jam' in *Selected Poems* by Jenny Bornholdt, © 2016 Victoria University Press, used by permission of Jenny Bornholdt and Te Herenga Waka University Press; quotation from 'Listening to the River' in *Selected Poems* by Brian Turner, © 2019 Victoria University Press, used by permission of Brian Turner and Te Herenga Waka University Press; quotation from 'Ohakune Fires' in *New and Selected Poems* by Lauris Edmond, © 1991 Oxford University Press, used by permission of Katherine Edmond; quotation from 'To a Sensitive Person' in *For Someone I Love – A Collection of Writing by Arapera Blank,* © 2015 Anton Blank Ltd, used by permission of Anton Blank; quotation from 'On the Road' in *Ruth Dallas: Collected Poems* by Ruth Dallas, © 1987 Otago University Press, used by permission of Hannah Brady and Otago University Press; quotation from 'Hope' in *Water, Leaves, Stones* by Dinah Hawken, © 1995 Otago University Press, used by permission of Dinah Hawken and Otago University Press; quotation from 'Miss Dust Lies in the Grass with Lennox' from *Miss Dust* by Johanna Aitchison, © 2015 Seraph Press, used by permission of Johanna Aitchison and Seraph Press; quotation from 'Starlings and History' by Charles Doyle, from *Landfall,* © 1956 *Landfall,* used by permission of Kegan Doyle and Otago University Press.

The following authors and others whose work I've drawn on, and who have helped me in other ways: Matt Merritt, Simon Barnes, Paul Vennell, Matt Gaw, Sophie Leguil, Catherine Knight, Jason

Pilkington, Juliet Batten, Fred Pearce, and Cherie Jacobson of the Katherine Mansfield House and Garden. A work not cited, but very influential on this book, is Katherine Swift's *The Morville Hours*.

Every effort has been made to trace copyright owners. The author would be grateful to hear of any errors or omissions. Any mistakes are the author's.

Some parts of this book appeared as abridged versions in *Ark* (Dark Mountain, UK); loveinthetimeofcovidchronicle.com; *Headland*; and the New Zealand Society of Authors Central Districts summer essay competition. Thank you to those publications and organisations whose acknowledgment of my work gave me the confidence to write this book.

The beautiful cover image is *Night Flight*, a reduction linocut by Julie Moonlight. Julie says: 'In 2020, and for some of 2021, we were unusually restricted to our "bubbles", and required to socially distance from other people or places. My images capture the freedom of life without boundaries that birds and nature continued to enjoy, without fear of this unseen enemy. *Night Flight* reflects my experience of being out in the bush at night, and conveys the different forms I see: the woven patterns of leaves, vines and branches, and wildlife as it goes about its business of living. They are symbols of life and freedom.'

Photographs on chapter-opening pages were taken by the author, with the exception of 'Summer'. The image for 'Winter' shows 'Tonga' (2000), a sculpture of carved Taranaki andesite by Filipe Tohi in Te Marae o Hine/The Square, Palmerston North.

# Notes

## Prologue

1.  Katherine Mansfield to Ida Baker, 7 March 1922, in *The Collected Letters of Katherine Mansfield: Volume 5: 1922–1923*, eds Vincent O'Sullivan and Margaret Scott (Oxford: Oxford University Press, 2008), p. 92.

## Soil

1.  Patricia Grace, 'Waiariki' in *Waiariki and Other Stories* (Auckland: Penguin, 2002), p. 33.
2.  'Pātaka kai free open street pantries', Pātaka Kai Open Street Pantries: www.patakai.co.nz
3.  David Malouf, 'The new loaf', in *An Open Book* (St Lucia: University of Queensland Press, 2018), p. 33.
4.  Adam Przywara, 'Ecologies of resilience: Westminster's bomb crater garden and the Dig for Victory campaign', *Seismopolite Journal of Art and Politics* (22 October 2016): www.seismopolite.com/ecologies-of-resilience-westminsters-bomb-crater-garden-and-the-dig-for-victory-campaign
5.  The original newspaper has composted into the garden but this article is available online at Wally Richards, 'Rain at last', *The Tribune*: www.gardenews.co.nz/page3.htm
6.  Simon Barnes, *The Meaning of Birds* (New York: Pegasus, 2018), p. 145.

7.  Les Molloy, *Soils in the New Zealand Landscape* (Lincoln: New Zealand Society of Soil Science, 1998), ch. 6: nzsss.science.org.nz/app/uploads/2016/03/soils_in_the_new_zealand_landscape_Contents.pdf
8.  James B. Nardi, *Life in the Soil* (Chicago: University of Chicago Press, 2007), pp. 47–49.
9.  Jessica Hutchings, Jo Smith and Garth Harmsworth, 'Elevating the mana of soil through the Hua Parakore Framework', *Mai Journal* 7(1), 2018, p. 94.
10. Te Ahukaramū Charles Royal, 'Papatūānuku – the land – The importance of Papatūānuku', *Te Ara – the Encyclopedia of New Zealand*: www.TeAra.govt.nz/en/papatuanuku-the-land/page-1
11. Basil Keane, 'Oneone – soils', *Te Ara – the Encyclopedia of New Zealand*: www.TeAra.govt.nz/en/oneone-soils
12. Hutchings, Smith and Harmsworth, 'Elevating the mana of soil', p. 98.

## Fungi

1.  Basil Dowling, 'Mushrooms', in *Canterbury and Other Poems* (Christchurch: The Caxton Press, 1949), p. 19.
2.  Suzanne Simard, David Perry, Melanie Jones, David Myrold, Daniel Durall and Randy Molinak, 'Net transfer of carbon between ectomycorrhizal tree species in the field', *Nature* 388, 1997, pp. 579–82.

3. Sylvia Plath, 'Mushrooms', in *The Colossus* (London: Faber & Faber, 1967), p. 34.
4. Tina White, 'Memory lane: Settler developed Massey land', *Manawatu Standard*, 8 February 2015: www.stuff.co.nz/manawatu-standard/lifestyle/65916176/memory-lane-settler-developed-massey-land
5. Chris Hyde, '"Oasis of calm" a groundsman's gift', *Manawatu Standard*, 29 December 2012: www.stuff.co.nz/manawatu-standard/news/8128168/Oasis-of-calm-a-groundsmans-gift
6. 'Massey University's gardens – A legacy of commitment to beauty', *Massey Focus* 3, Spring 1991: https://tamiro.massey.ac.nz/nodes/view/1748#idx14265

## Fruit

1. Jenny Bornholdt, 'Peach, the Jam', in *Selected Poems* (Wellington: Victoria University Press, 2016), p. 138.
2. 'Employment and rationing', National Archives: www.nationalarchives.gov.uk/cabinetpapers/themes/employment-rationing.htm
3. 'New Zealand wartime food (WWII)', Cook's Info, 5 May 2011: www.cooksinfo.com/new-zealand-wartime-food
4. Wikipedia, 'Feijoa sellowiana': https://en.wikipedia.org/wiki/Feijoa_sellowiana
5. Jacinda Ardern, Level 2 announcement, Beehive, 11 May 2020: www.beehive.govt.nz/speech/level-2-announcement

## Water

1. Brian Turner, 'Listening to the River', in *Selected Poems* (Wellington: Victoria University Press, 2019), p. 42.

2. 'Badvertising – stop adverts fuelling the climate emergency', *New Weather Institute*, 3 August 2020: www.newweather.org/2020/08/03/badvertising-stop-adverts-fuelling-the-climate-emergency
3. Juliet Batten, *Celebrating the Southern Seasons: Rituals for Aotearoa* (Auckland: Random House, 2005), p. 30.
4. Fiona Harvey, 'World has six months to avert climate crisis, says energy expert', *Guardian*, 18 June 2020: www.theguardian.com/environment/2020/jun/18/world-has-six-months-to-avert-climate-crisis-says-energy-expert
5. Malcolm McKinnon, 'Manawatū and Horowhenua places – Manawatū River and Gorge', *Te Ara – the Encyclopedia of New Zealand*: www.TeAra.govt.nz/en/manawatu-and-horowhenua-places/page-6
6. Jon Morgan and Kelly Burns, 'Manawatu River "among worst in the West"', *Dominion Post*, 2 December 2009: www.stuff.co.nz/environment/3097651/Manawatu-River-among-worst-in-the-West
7. 'The Manawatū river flows through all of us. It is precious because it is ours', The Manawatū River Leaders' Accord: www.manawaturiver.co.nz
8. Chris McDowall and Tim Denee, *We Are Here* (Auckland: Massey University Press, 2019), p. 217.
9. Mathew Grocott, 'River "should be safe for children"', *Manawatu Standard*, 7 June 2011: www.stuff.co.nz/manawatu-standard/news/5107070/River-should-be-safe-for-children
10. Catherine Knight, *Ravaged Beauty* (New Zealand: Tōtara Press, 2018), pp. 175–95.

## Star

1. Lauris Edmond, 'Ohakune Fires', in *New and Selected Poems* (Auckland: Oxford University Press, 1991), pp. 15–16.
2. Paul Meredith, 'Matariki – Te Tau Hou Māori', *Te Ara – the Encyclopedia of New Zealand*: www.TeAra.govt.nz/en/matariki-maori-new-year
3. Paul Meredith, 'Matariki – Te Tau Hou Māori – Cycles of life and death', *Te Ara – the Encyclopedia of New Zealand*: www.TeAra.govt.nz/en/matariki-te-tau-hou-maori/page-2
4. Martin Rees, 'Templeton Prize 2011: Full transcript of Martin Rees's acceptance speech', *Guardian*, 6 April 2011: www.theguardian.com/science/2011/apr/06/templeton-prize-2011-martin-rees-speech
5. Wikipedia, 'Lighting': https://en.wikipedia.org/wiki/Lighting
6. Robert Louis Stevenson, quoted in Tom Moriarty, 'The illuminating history of lighting', *English Heritage*, 6 November 2017: http://blog.english-heritage.org.uk/history-of-lighting
7. Mary Bellis, 'The history of lighting and lamps', *ThoughtCo.*, 2 July 2019: www.thoughtco.com/history-of-lighting-and-lamps-1992089
8. Katherine Mansfield to Elizabeth von Arnim, Countess Russell, 16 October 1922, in *The Collected Letters of Katherine Mansfield: Volume 4: 1920–1921*, eds Vincent O'Sullivan and Margaret Scott (Oxford: Clarendon Press, 1996), p. 297.
9. Matt Gaw, 'In a bad light', *Resurgence and Ecologist* 323, November/December 2020, pp. 32–34.
10. 'Journey through the stars', Palmerston North City Council, 3 February 2020: www.pncc.govt.nz/news-events/news/journey-through-the-stars
11. 'New star path lights up the Manawatū River', Palmerston North City Council, 16 October 2020: www.pncc.govt.nz/News-Events/News/Palmys-new-Star-Path-lights-up-the-Manawatū-River
12. Mason Durie and Meihana Durie, 'The origins of Rangitāne', *Te Ara – the Encyclopedia of New Zealand*: www.TeAra.govt.nz/en/rangitane/page-1

## Stone

1. A.R.D. Fairburn, 'Elements', in *Collected Poems* (Christchurch: Pegasus, 1966), p. 27.
2. George Petersen, *The Pioneering Days of Palmerston North* (Levin: n.p., 1952), p. 69.
3. Information about Whātonga is from the interpretation sign in Manawatū Gorge and from 'Whatonga, Captain of the Kurahaupo Waka', Geni, 26 October 2019: www.geni.com/people/Whatonga-Captain-of-the-Kurahaupo-Waka/6000000013496999334
4. Information about Te Au Rere a Te Tonga is from the interpretation sign in Manawatū Gorge and from Michele Frey, *Te Āpiti – Manawatū Gorge Te Au-rere-a-te-tonga. A History* (Palmerston North: Te Āpiti Governance Group, Horizons Regional Council, 2019), pp. 13–14.
5. Dorothy Pilkington, *Terrace End Cemetery Walk* (Palmerston North: Friends of Terrace End Cemetery, 1995), pp. 2–26: www.interment.net/data/

nz/wanganui_manawatu/terrace_end/
terrace-end-cemetery-walk-booklet.pdf

6.  Information about Memorial Park
    is from the interpretation sign in
    Memorial Park and from Jason
    Pilkington, Memorial Park guided tour,
    3 November 2020.

7.  Wikisource, 'We have fed you all for a
    thousand years': https://en.wikisource.
    org/wiki/Songs_of_the_Workers_
    (15th_edition)/We_Have_Fed_You_
    All_for_a_Thousand_Years

## Blossom

1.  Arapera Hineira Kaa Blank, 'To a
    Sensitive Person', in *For Someone I Love
    – A Collection of Writing* by Arapera
    Blank (Auckland: Anton Blank Ltd,
    2015) p. 41.

2.  Juliet Batten, *Celebrating the Southern
    Seasons: Rituals for Aotearoa* (Auckland:
    Random House, 2005), p. 106.

3.  Rowan McOnegal, 'Elderflower –
    power and protection', 28 October
    2018: https://hedgerowmedicine.org/
    blog/2018/10/8/elderflower-power-and-
    protection

4.  'US West Coast fires: I don't think
    science knows about climate, says
    Trump', BBC, 15 September 2020:
    www.bbc.com/news/world-us-
    canada-54144651

5.  Tim Flannery, 'The megafires and
    pandemic expose the lies that frustrate
    action on climate change', *Guardian*,
    16 September 2020: www.theguardian.
    com/australia-news/2020/sep/17/the-
    megafires-and-pandemic-expose-the-
    lies-that-frustrate-action-on-climate-
    change

6.  'New Zealand bushfire that demolished
    village leads to climate crisis debate',
    *Guardian*, 6 October 2020: www.
    theguardian.com/world/2020/oct/06/
    new-zealand-bushfire-that-demolished-
    village-leads-to-climate-crisis-debate

7.  Joanna Orwin, 'Shrubs and small trees
    of the forest – Lookalike subcanopy
    trees', *Te Ara – the Encyclopedia of
    New Zealand*: www.TeAra.govt.nz/en/
    shrubs-and-small-trees-of-the-forest/
    page-2

8.  Batten, *Celebrating the Southern
    Seasons*, p. 20.

## Bird

1.  Mary Ursula Bethell, 'The Long Harbour',
    in *Time and Place* (Christchurch: The
    Caxton Press, 1936), p. 12.

2.  Jonathan O'Callaghan, 'What are
    those strange moving lights in the
    night sky? Elon Musk's "Starlink"
    satellites explained', *Forbes*, 21
    April 2020: www.forbes.com/sites/
    jonathanocallaghan/2020/04/21/
    what-are-those-strange-moving-lights-
    in-the-night-sky-elon-musks-starlink-
    satellites-explained

3.  Simon Barnes, *The Meaning of Birds*
    (New York: Pegasus Press, 2018), pp.
    142–53.

4.  James Gorman, 'It could be the Age of
    the Chicken, geologically', *New York
    Times*, 11 December 2018: www.nytimes.
    com/2018/12/11/science/chicken-
    anthropocene-archaeology.html

5.  Barnes, *The Meaning of Birds*, pp.
    142–53.

6.  Laura Spinney, 'Is factory farming to
    blame for the coronavirus?', *Guardian*,

28 March 2020: www.theguardian.com/
world/2020/mar/28/is-factory-farming-
to-blame-for-coronavirus

7. Sian Anna Lewis, 'Britain's official
bird is announced', *BBC Countryfile*,
6 November 2015: https://www.
countryfile.com/wildlife/britains-
official-bird-is-announced

8. 'Jean-François Millet: *The Gleaners*
– 1857', Great Works of Western
Art: www.worldsbestpaintings.net/
artistsandpaintings/painting/103

9. Barnes, *The Meaning of Birds*, p. 294.

10. Gordon Ell, *Enjoying Nature in the New
Zealand Garden* (Auckland: The Bush
Press, 1993), p. 29.

11. 'Manawatu Estuary', National
Wetland Trust of New Zealand: www.
wetlandtrust.org.nz/get-involved/
ramsar-wetlands/manawatu-estuary

12. Daniel Boffey, '"Jet fighter" godwit
breaks world record for non-stop bird
flight', *Guardian*, 13 October 2020:
www.theguardian.com/
environment/2020/oct/13/jet-fighter-
godwit-breaks-world-record-for-non-
stop-bird-flight

13. Batten, *Celebrating the Southern
Seasons*, p. 25.

14. Matt Merritt, *A Sky Full of Birds*
(London: Rider, 2016), p. 44.

15. 'Pīpīwharauroa Shining Cuckoo', Bird
of the Year: www.birdoftheyear.org.nz/
shining-cuckoo

16. David Hambling, 'Weatherwatch:
Beltane celebrates cleansing power of
returning sun', *Guardian*, 1 May 2020:
www.theguardian.com/news/2020/
may/01/weatherwatch-beltane-celebrates-
cleansing-power-of-returning-sun; Batten,
*Celebrating the Southern Seasons*, p. 135.

## Wind

1. Ruth Dallas, 'On the Road', in *Ruth
Dallas: Collected Poems* (Dunedin:
Otago University Press, 1987), p. 74.

2. J.D. Cowie, 'Loess in the Manawatu
District, New Zealand', *New Zealand
Journal of Geology and Geophysics* 7(2),
1964, pp. 389–96: www.tandfonline.
com/doi/pdf/10.1080/00288306.1964.
10420185

3. Matt McGlone, 'Evolution of plants
and animals – How did they arrive?' *Te
Ara – the Encyclopedia of New Zealand*:
www.TeAra.govt.nz/en/shrubs-and-
small-trees-of-the-forest/page-2

4. 'About Monarch butterflies', World
Wildlife Fund: wwf.ca/species/
monarch-butterfly

5. Information about Memorial Park is
from Jason Pilkington, Memorial Park
guided tour, 3 November 2020.

6. William Butler Yeats, 'To a child dancing
in the wind', in *Responsibilities and Other
Poems* (New York: Macmillan, 1916),
p. 66.

7. Basil Keane, 'Tāwhirimātea – the
weather – Origins of the weather', *Te
Ara – the Encyclopedia of New Zealand*:
www.TeAra.govt.nz/en/tawhirimatea-
the-weather/page-1

8. Grant Miller, 'Council culls 60 geese at
lagoon', *Manawatu Standard*, 20 January
2011: www.stuff.co.nz/manawatu-
standard/news/4560643/Council-culls-
60-geese-at-lagoon

9. Adina Bresge, 'The rise of Canada
geese: How the birds bounced back
from near extinction', Associated Press,
30 June 2020: https://globalnews.
ca/news/7124540/canada-geese-
extinction/#:~:text=Prior%20to%20

European%20colonization%2C%20
the,extinctio%20from%20these%20
native%20habitats

10. Juliet Batten, *Celebrating the Southern Seasons: Rituals for Aotearoa* (Auckland: Random House, 2005), p. 134.

11. "'This is a country of possibilities": Kamala Harris's speech in full', Guardian, 8 November 2020: www.theguardian.com/us-news/2020/nov/08/this-is-a-country-of-possibilities-kamala-harriss-speech-in-full

12. Catherine Knight, *Ravaged Beauty* (New Zealand: Tōtara Press, 2018), p. 237.

## Tree

1. Dinah Hawken, 'Hope', in *Water, Leaves, Stones* (Wellington: Victoria University Press, 1995), p. 74.

2. Robert Vennell, *The Meaning of Trees* (Auckland: Harper Collins, 2019), pp. 13–14.

3. Kennedy Warne, 'The future of our forests', *New Zealand Geographic*, July–August, 2014: www.nzgeo.com/stories/the-future-of-our-forests

4. Catherine Knight, *Beyond Manapouri* (Christchurch: Canterbury University Press, 2018), p. 205.

5. Catherine Knight, *Wildbore – A Photographic Legacy* (New Zealand: Tōtara Press, 2018), p. 71.

6. Vennell, *The Meaning of Trees*, p. 19.

7. Te Ahukaramū Charles Royal, 'Te Waonui a Tāne – forest mythology – Sayings from the forest', *Te Ara – the Encyclopedia of New Zealand*: www.TeAra.govt.nz/en/te-waonui-a-tane-forest-mythology/page-5

8. Vennell, *The Meaning of Trees*, p. 129.

9. Tina White, 'Memory lane: Settler developed Massey land', *Manawatu Standard*, 8 February 2015: www.stuff.co.nz/manawatu-standard/lifestyle/65916176/memory-lane-settler-developed-massey-land

10. Maggy Wassilieff, 'Tall broadleaf trees – Coastal trees', *Te Ara – the Encyclopedia of New Zealand*: www.TeAra.govt.nz/en/weeds-of-agriculture/page-1

11. Information about the karaka grove is from the interpretation board at the site and from 'Dawn blessing for Karaka Grove', Massey University, 14 December 2016: www.massey.ac.nz/massey/about-massey/news/article.cfm?mnarticle_uuid=C2AA4F15-BE01-0964-8207-98124A241D41

12. 'He Ara Kotahi', Palmerston North City Council: www.pncc.govt.nz/services/parks-venues-recreation/walks-and-walkways/he-ara-kotahi

13. Margaret Forster, guided tour of He Ara Kotahi, 16 April 2021.

14. 'The "great" conjunction of Jupiter and Saturn', NASA, 16 December 2020: www.nasa.gov/feature/the-great-conjunction-of-jupiter-and-saturn

15. Wikipedia, 'Great conjunction': https://en.wikipedia.org/wiki/Great_conjunction#Notable_great_conjunctions

16. 'Pinus radiata', Royal Botanic Garden Edinburgh: https://threatenedconifers.rbge.org.uk/conifers/pinus-radiata; 'History of New Zealand from 1200', McGuinness Institute: www.mcguinnessinstitute.org/about/the-james-duncan-reference-library/history-of-new-zealand-from-1200

17. Eloise Gibson, 'The unpopular tree sucking carbon from our air', Newsroom, 9 September 2019: www.newsroom.co.nz/nobody-loves-radiata
18. Adam Forbes, David Norton and Fiona Carswell, 'Opportunities and limitations of exotic *Pinus radiata* as a facilitative nurse for New Zealand Indigenous forest restoration', *New Zealand Journal of Forestry Science* 49(6), 2019, p. 1.
19. Warne, 'The future of our forests'.
20. 'Wilding conifers', Department of Conservation: www.doc.govt.nz/nature/pests-and-threats/weeds/common-weeds/wilding-conifers
21. Jason Pilkington, guided tour of Memorial Park, 3 November 2020.

## Weed

1. Johanna Aitchison, 'Miss Dust lies on the lawn with Lennox', in *Miss Dust* (Wellington: Seraph Press, 2015), p. 32.
2. Barbara Smith, '9 ways to win the war on oxalis', *Stuff*, 3 August 2016: www.stuff.co.nz/life-style/homed/garden/82791116/q--a-how-can-i-get-rid-of-oxalis
3. Ian Popay, 'Weeds of agriculture – Introduction of weeds', *Te Ara – the Encyclopedia of New Zealand*: www.TeAra.govt.nz/en/weeds-of-agriculture/page-1
4. Alex Morss, '"Not just weeds": How rebel botanists are using graffiti to name forgotten flora', *Guardian*, 1 May 2020: www.theguardian.com/environment/2020/may/01/not-just-weeds-how-rebel-botanists-are-using-graffiti-to-name-forgotten-flora-aoe
5. Sophie Leguil, 'A history of weeding', *More than Weeds*, https://morethanweeds.co.uk/a-history-of-weeding
6. Wikipedia, 'Glyphosate': https://en.wikipedia.org/wiki/Glyphosate
7. Leguil, 'A history of weeding'.
8. Wikipedia, 'Damned yellow composite': https://en.wikipedia.org/wiki/Damned_yellow_composite
9. Wikipedia, 'Asteraceae': https://en.wikipedia.org/wiki/Asteraceae
10. Morss, '"Not just weeds"'.
11. 'Shrinking biodiversity poses major risk to the future of global food and agriculture, landmark UN report shows', United Nations, 22 February 2019: https://news.un.org/en/story/2019/02/1033331
12. 'The new wild: Why invasive species will be nature's salvation', Massey University Political Ecology Research Centre: https://perc.ac.nz/wordpress/the-new-wild-why-invasive-species-will-be-natures-salvation
13. Maggy Wassilieff, 'Tall broadleaf trees – Coastal trees', *Te Ara – the Encyclopedia of New Zealand*: www.TeAra.govt.nz/en/weeds-of-agriculture/page-1

## Insect

1. Anne Glenny Wilson, 'A spring afternoon in New Zealand', in *A New Zealand Verse*, eds W.F. Alexander and A.E. Currie (Walter Scott, 1906), p. 39.
2. Caspar Hallmann, Martin Sorg, Eelke Jongejans, Henk Siepel, Nick Hofland, Heinz Schwan, Werner Stenmans, Andreas Müller, Hubert Sumser, Thomas Hörren, Dave Goulson and

Hans de Kroon, 'More than 75 percent decline over 27 years in total flying insect biomass in protected areas', *PLoS ONE* 12(10), 2017.

3. 'Honey bees brought to New Zealand', Ministry for Culture and Heritage, updated 8 October 2020: https://nzhistory.govt.nz/mary-bumby-brings-the-first-honey-bees-in-new-zealand

4. University of California – Berkeley, 'Pollinators help one-third of the world's food crop production', *ScienceDaily*, 26 October 2006: www.sciencedaily.com/releases/2006/10/061025165904.htm

5. Robert Billens, *From Swamp to City: Official souvenir 1887–1937: Commemorating the Diamond Jubilee of the city* (Palmerston North: K. & B. Print, 1937), p. 25.

6. John Marris, 'Cicadas – Life cycle and enemies', *Te Ara – the Encyclopedia of New Zealand*: www.TeAra.govt.nz/en/cicadas/page-2

## Epilogue

1. Charles Doyle, 'Starlings and History', *Landfall* 38, 1956, pp. 92–94.

**KA HAEA TE ATA** is the first line of a Kāi Tahu karakia that welcomes the new day.

Published by Otago University Press
Te Whare Tā o Te Wānanga o Ōtākou
533 Castle Street
Dunedin, New Zealand
university.press@otago.ac.nz
www.oup.nz/press

First published 2024
Text copyright © Miriam Sharland

ISBN 978-1-99004870-8

Published with the assistance of Creative New Zealand.

ARTS COUNCIL OF NEW ZEALAND TOI AOTEAROA

Editor: Jane Parkin
Design: Fiona Moffat
Typesetting: Mel Stevens
Cover artwork: Julie Moonlight, *Night Flight*, 2021 (four-colour reduction linocut, 305 x 305mm)
Cover image photographer: Abigail Moonlight

Printed in Aotearoa New Zealand by Ligare.